D0855089

TIME'S COVENANT

TIME'S COVENANT

THE ESSAYS AND SERMONS

OF WILLIAM CLANCY

Eugene Green, Editor

University of Pittsburgh Press

Published by the University of Pittsburgh Press,
Pittsburgh, Pa., 15260
Copyright © 1987, University of Pittsburgh Press
All rights reserved
Feffer and Simons, Inc., London
Manufactured in the United States of America

Library of Congress Cataloging-in-Publication Data

Clancy, William, 1922–1981.
    Time's covenant.

    1. Catholic Church — Doctrines.   2. Catholic
Church — Sermons.   3. Sermons, American.   I. Green,
Eugene, 1944–   .   II. Title.
BX1755.C58   1987   282'.73   86-19517
ISBN 0-8229-3545-7

Contents

SERMONS

Introduction

BY MICHAEL MORAN

■ *Commonweal* has been at the center of American Catholic intellectual life since the first issue was published in 1924. According to Rodger Van Allen, in *"The Commonweal" and American Catholicism*, the journal in its early years was a literary, heavily churchy magazine, intellectually attuned to Anglo-American and European Catholic interests. As *Commonweal* grew, however, it became increasingly attached to developing Catholic cultural, intellectual, political, and social movements in the United States. Van Allen gives credit to *Commonweal* for guiding these movements toward maturity. The magazine in many ways provided a clarion call to immigrant American Catholics to relinquish their defensive ghettoism and to accept full participation in American intellectual, social, and cultural life.

When William Clancy joined *Commonweal* in 1952, the journal, unlike the American Catholic hierarchy and the Catholic press in general, had taken a strong position against Senator Joseph McCarthy and his grim crusade against Communists. John Cooney, in *An American Pope*, writes that Cardinal Spellman, for example, publicly supported both McCarthy and his tactics. Many prominent Catholic periodicals equated pro-McCarthyism with being a good Catholic, since the Roman Catholic Church had condemned communism as evil; conversely, opponents of McCarthy were *ipso facto* anti-Catholic. To a large extent because of *Commonweal*'s relentless attacks on McCarthyism, its writers came to be known as "liberal Catholics," and the magazine itself was highly suspect among conservative Catholics.

Clancy entered this atmosphere at *Commonweal* following a rather astonishing experience at the University of Notre Dame. As an instructor in the English department, he was immensely popular with both faculty and students. He wanted an academic career and was in the process of completing his Ph.D. degree at the University of Michigan. During his second year at Notre Dame, Cardinal Spellman issued a pastoral letter condemning as immoral Roberto Rossellini's film *The Miracle*, which apparently the cardinal had never seen. *Commonweal* disagreed with Cardinal Spellman and took an editorial position advocating cultural freedom in a pluralistic society. The magazine also published Clancy's article "The Catholic as Philistine" in which he attacked the attempted censorship by Spellman and others as "semi-ecclesiastic McCarthyism." Clancy was summarily fired from his teaching position at Notre Dame. No official explanation was offered, but Clancy learned unofficially that his article was the cause of his dismissal. He once reported that seven years later he was in Chicago having a drink with Frank O'Malley, the legendary professor of writing at Notre Dame. O'Malley, according to Clancy, confirmed his suspicion that Cardinal Spellman had phoned the president of Notre Dame and demanded that Clancy be dismissed because of his "anti-Catholic attitudes." Although angry at the time of his humiliating treatment by Notre Dame, Clancy came eventually to express genuine gratitude and appreciation for the cardinal, whose action resulted in his move from South Bend to New York.

Together with other *Commonweal* editors of the 1950s, notably John Cogley, James O'Gara, Edward Skillin, and James

Finn, William Clancy made substantial contributions to the articulation of the liberal Catholic tradition, to the defense of freedom of expression in all the arts and in politics, and to the shaping and defending of the position that cherished American freedom and the presence of the Roman Catholic Church need not be incompatible. In those pre-Vatican II days *Commonweal* displayed consistent courage and foresight in its efforts to modify through enlightenment the prevailing siege mentality of so many Catholics, a mentality which in the 1950s seemed at times to reach a level of paranoia.

In *A Canterbury Tale* John Cogley points out that while he was an editor of *Commonweal*, "there was such a creature as a 'Commonweal Catholic'" who was "considered to be outside the pale." There was apparently no concensual definition of the term, but Cogley asserts that it was applied to those who "criticized Senator Joseph McCarthy, gave unfavorable reviews to Cardinal Spellman's novel, and took a dim view of the Legion of Decency's moral simplicity." Commonweal Catholics were not Catholic enough because they were intellectually liberated from a "largely self-imposed ghettoism." Commonweal editors "did not go along with the dominant mood in either Church or state; consequently, we were held in widespread disrepute by both." Nevertheless, "as far as our own Catholicity went, we were incurable essentialists."

William Clancy was unquestionably a Commonweal Catholic, especially in the sense that he was an ardent civil libertarian, but never a radical. In conversation he frequently alluded to James Madison's belief that history had shown that more human freedoms were eroded by gradual and quiet encroachments of those in power than by violent, abrupt upheavals. This theme can be discerned in some of his best *Commonweal* essays. He believed that efforts to abridge essential human freedoms, whether it be the work of individuals, church, or state, must be exposed and resisted; otherwise, civilized life is impossible. He called for "critical sanity" in the face of threats to cultural and artistic freedom, and in an essay in *Commonweal* in October 1952, he warned that "informed opinion in the United States must be loud in its continuous insistence on the basically pluralistic structure of our society, and hence quick to defend those accused of 'subversion' merely because of their failure to conform to majority patterns of thought or behavior. It must encourage the growth of variety and nonconformity in our cultural patterns, because these are essential to a free society." He clearly understood and feared the dangers of both right-wing authoritarianism and "naive liberalism."

Clancy's lifelong liberal interest in human freedom was markedly different from a liberalism or libertarianism which enfranchises individuals to do whatever they please as long as they do not impede the rights of others. He was interested in guaranteed civil rights because he valued civility in human relationships. He believed that true civility was possible only in a society that was organized around a core of commonly accepted laws and principles, guaranteed civil rights and, of course, good public manners. In this regard he valued highly the Chair of Peter and the Crown of England because he perceived in both symbols a powerful civilizing potential that invited men and women to transcend human weakness and the tawdriness that characterize much daily life. As a Christian realist, however, he believed that it was only through grace that men and women can transcend their human limitations.

In act 2 of *Iolanthe*, W. S. Gilbert includes a verse that describes a comical certainty:

> That every boy and every gal
> That's born into the world alive
> Is either a little Liberal
> Or else a little Conservative!

William Clancy was both. During the 1950s when he was an editor of *Commonweal*, he was widely known and respected as a liberal Catholic writer and journalist. But in time he came to resent the liberal designation because he understood, correctly, that his liberalism was significantly different from the conventional liberal ideology embraced most consistently by the American Democratic party. He never, for example, shared Franklin Delano Roosevelt's belief in the wisdom and efficacy of the will of the majority, nor did he ever endorse Roosevelt's contention that the government can best insure the freedom and happiness of individuals by meeting all social problems with new social controls. Although clearly a liberal, Clancy did not identify with the liberal tradition born in the seventeenth and eighteenth centuries in the writings of Rousseau, Locke, Hobbes, and Hume; he strongly disapproved of the emphasis this tradition placed on rationalism and its celebration of individualistic skepticism. The philosophical basis for his liberalism was derived instead from Aristotle, Erasmus, Thomas Aquinas, Thomas More, and more recently Lord Acton, all of whom he had read carefully during his undergraduate days at the Jesuit University of Detroit. His thoughts also reflected the influence of Jacques Maritain, Etienne Gilson, Baron von Hügel, and Georges Bernanos.

Given the intellectual roots of his liberalism, he preferred to be known as a Christian liberal or a Commonweal liberal. His liberal attitudes were attached to a Christian humanistic tradition, a tradition which included a theistic view of the world and which emphasized personalism and human freedom, but always within the context of a shared history and heritage dominated by the inescapable need of humans for communal life.

Though sometimes it was misunderstood as such, Clancy's liberalism was never naive. In an editorial following Adlai Stevenson's failed bid for the presidency in 1952, he wrote that Stevenson might have restored to American politics "the finest element of genuine liberalism: its value for the tentative judgment, its rejection of political dogmatism." He consistently emphasized the moral, intellectual, and spiritual basis of the liberal vision; he understood that not all liberals are "liberal" and could be just as menacing to civilized political discourse as dogmatic reactionaries.

In Adlai Stevenson, William Clancy recognized those "gentlemanly virtues" that were part of the liberal humanist tradition he cherished and lived by. Stevenson was a sophisticated, detached, and intelligent man; but above all he was a gentleman, a truly honorable and decent man. Reading the essays in this volume, it seems reasonable to infer that Clancy reacted strongly to the tenor, character, and style of a politician. He expressed less interest in substantive political issues; these, after all, varied in gravity and were for the most part transitory. For him the important element in political life was character, much more important than political ideology or party affiliation. After all, he seemed to argue, men of strong character, such as Stevenson, could be expected to behave well in office and engage the challenges of political issues in an honorable and decent manner. It was this attitude toward politics that permitted him to admire deeply such diverse political figures as Lord Melbourne, Winston Churchill, Charles de Gaulle, and Helmut Schmidt. As common denominators, all these politicians possessed strong character, intelligence, and prudence in government. He was appalled by the New Left of the 1960s because of its relentless assault on those civilizing values he most cherished; the exuberance and self-righteousness of the American political Right was equally repugnant to him.

G. K. Chesterton once wrote that the truly tolerant man is able to accept all viewpoints because he has none of his own; but the liberalism Clancy embraced recognized an overarching central truth about humanity and its destiny. This revealed truth and the tradition it generated had the ultimate effect of encouraging thoughtful individuals to be more humble and necessarily more tolerant of diversity in a pluralistic society. *Commonweal* liberals affirm the dignity of all human life and perceive this dignity as emanating from the mystery inherent in human life and the presence of divine grace by which humanity is saved. For Clancy, Christian liberalism was mostly concerned with relationships: our relationship to God and to each other in community life.

William Clancy chose to be a liberal Catholic because he recognized the shortcomings and dangers of conservative Catholicism as he understood it. He believed that conservative Catholics embraced a "tragically parochial view of history and religion" and in so doing risked placing themselves outside history. He perceived in the conservative Catholic philosophy an antidemocratic spirit which seemed to lend support to "majoritarian Catholicism" with the inexorable consequences of "coercion, censorship, and suppression." Clancy understood the absurdity of the conservative Catholic's implied desire to abandon the twentieth century; he wrote that we "must live in the modern world, and it is this world which we must save, for he [the liberal Catholic] reminds his 'conservative' friends that we can have no other."

In many ways, much like Chesterton, William Clancy led a life of practical romance; the world of sin and folly was much with him, but he was a gracious and high-minded gentleman. He trusted his generous gift of imagination to instruct him on important matters. Similarly, his love of poetry reflected much more than aesthetic delight; he once told me that whatever large and small truths he possessed, most had been acquired by reading the great poets.

In 1961, Clancy left New York to study theology at Oxford

University. He was ordained a Roman Catholic priest in 1964. From 1968 until his death in 1982 at the age of fifty-nine, he was pastor of the University Oratory of the Holy Spirit Parish and provost of the Oratory community in Pittsburgh. This non-geographical parish was established in 1967 to serve the students, faculty, and staff at three adjoining educational institutions: the University of Pittsburgh, Carnegie-Mellon University, and Chatham College. Father Clancy became known as a wise and sensitive confessor and counselor who taught his penitents to be charitable toward themselves. But above all he was widely acclaimed as a brilliant preacher of the Good News. He was a joyous Easter Christian who never lost sight of the irreducibly tragic side of life. (Often he re-read the works of Nicholas Berdyaev and Miguel de Unamuno.) In the words of Paul Tillich, Father Clancy lived his life "doing the truth."

Although William Clancy became a Catholic priest, he never abandoned his intelligent, well-informed, and liberal philosophy. And yet he was a concerned theologian who had little patience with modern theological trends. Over the years his belief in God matured into profound and unshakable faith, a passionate intuition of a promised glory.

To speak of Father Clancy one must speak of his ruling passions: Bach and Mozart, New York and London, the Word and words, especially poetry. He read great poetry almost daily and had committed an astonishing number of poems to memory. Given to describing his interests and discoveries with superlatives, he sometimes referred to favorite poems as "theophanies." He often quoted Blake, Donne, Hopkins, Marvell, Rilke, and Eliot; he read and frequently reread the first epistle of Pope's "Essay on Man," and he created a special category for his beloved Yeats: the poet, it seemed to him, who best celebrated the dignity and immortality of man. Although he held degrees in English literature, Father Clancy had little fondness for academic literary criticism; he preferred to trust his remarkable, intuitive intelligence to guide him to the meanings and mysteries in poetic language. For him, poetry, and of course religion, were necessary in order to transcend what he regarded as the intolerable arrogance of scientific materialism with its limited grasp of a partial reality. His intellectual hero was John Henry Newman, and he shared Newman's distrust of the rationalist-scientific temperament.

Father Clancy had no technical training in music, but he listened to serious music every day, and he was a knowledgeable critic with an impressively discriminating ear. Stopping short of attributing epiphanic powers to great music, he nonetheless responded to sublime works, and especially to the music of Bach and Mozart, with an almost mystical admixture of awe and ecstasy, wonder and reverence. (He was genuinely saddened and bewildered by individuals who did not share his love for Bach and Mozart; similarly, he simply refused to believe that any civilized person would not love New York and London.)

In preparing young Oratorians for the priesthood, Father Clancy urged them not to preach from a prepared text. In all the years I knew him as a priest, I never once observed him mounting the pulpit with anything more than a few scribbled words, indicating broad topics he wanted to include in his homily. On occasion, in fact, he relished the challenge of preaching extempore, without having read the assigned scripture passages before the liturgy. When he did prepare a homily, his method was certainly unorthodox: he would first read scripture and then listen to Bach or Mozart; he rarely sought information from theology or other reference books. He was exceptionally well-educated in the humanities, and he had absorbed an immense fund of theological insights during his years of study at Oxford University. (He was profoundly influenced by Paul Tillich and Karl Barth.)

Once in the pulpit, Father Clancy seemed to be transmuted in a manner that demanded the complete attention of the congregation. The conflux of his presence, his deep, resonant voice, and his intellectual brilliance created a special ambience which suggested a real cooperation with divine grace. In fact, he was quite reluctant to take any credit for his accomplishments as a preacher; rather, he insisted that preaching for him was a mysterious activity which involved his becoming an instrument of God.

The influence of poetry and music is apparent in his best sermons, which might appropriately be described as hymnlike, free-verse celebrations of the presence and mystery of God. Father Clancy had a gift for choosing noble, poetic language, and his sermons frequently took on a musical cadence and structure as he explored Christian themes and paradoxes in a contrapuntal style that he inevitably resolved into a harmonious whole.

Father Clancy's Christology was securely located in the Trinitarian formula declared by the Council of Chalcedon in 451 A.D. He said in a sermon preached on the Feast of Candlemas in 1980: "All diversity in the Church must be weighed in the balance against the rock of the Church's faith . . . the faith proclaimed by John the Baptist: Behold the Son of God on whom God's favor rests. Behold the salvation of the nations. This Jesus is no mere creature. He is the Eternal Word. In Him shines forth the Glory of God." He added that any diversity in the Church which threatens this essential basis of the Catholic faith is not Catholic "and it is the Church's duty to say it is not Catholic."

Father Clancy had a profound belief that as a priest he did not express his own existence when he proclaimed the word of God. Nevertheless, he felt that in preaching he should reflect a personal reality — that he himself was gripped by the spirit of God. In this he invariably succeeded. He expressed the word of God and his love for Jesus the Christ with his Christian existence, and he believed that as a priest he should do this because the Church he loved must do this. All of us should attempt to imitate Christ, but the priest must make a special effort, for to him is given the word of God, and it is this gift that makes him a priest.

It is important for readers to keep in mind that the sermons in this volume are all transcribed from tapes. They record what Father Clancy said, not what he wrote. Indeed, not even the transcriptions were seen by Father Clancy, most of them having been made after his death. Moreover, most of the taped sermons were recorded during the last three years of his life. Some of the great sermons from earlier years are simply not available to us. But even in what little remains there appears the glimmer of a great spirit, greatly devoted to his task. Like the poets and preachers of a former time, men he admired such as John Donne and John Henry Newman, William Clancy, God's loyal ambassador, God's priest, preached the ineffable both movingly and eloquently.

ESSAYS

The Catholic as Philistine

■ The now celebrated crusade to suppress Rossellini's film, *The Miracle*, has followed closely upon two similar campaigns: the efforts to censor and suppress the Rutgers undergraduate magazine, *Antho*, for publishing a short story which certain elements in the local Catholic community considered "immoral" and "blasphemous," and the successful attempt to remove certain Charlie Chaplin comedies from movie and television screens in New Jersey because the Catholic War Veterans "suspected Chaplin of having Leftist sympathies." These three efforts have been attended by wide publicity, and the latest one, the battle over *The Miracle*, has been marked by particular bitterness on both sides.

The pattern of these campaigns has shocked thousands of non-Catholic Americans, and this shock is shared by many loyal Catholics. Our shock, however, is a deeper one than any that can be felt by our non-Catholic neighbors, for we have more at stake; we are profoundly disturbed to see certain of our coreligionists embarked upon crusades which we feel can result only in great harm to the cause of religion, of art, and of intelligence. These appeals to mass hysteria, these highly arbitrary invocations of a police censorship must ultimately result, we feel, in great harm to the cause of religion as well as art. They are, we feel, a most deplorable violation of the human spirit,

Commonweal, 16 March 1951; reprinted, 16 November 1973

a violation which will justly expose us to the enmity of many men of goodwill, and furnish ammunition to the enemies of the Church.

These three cases of *Antho*, the Charlie Chaplin films, and *The Miracle* have much in common; they form a pattern. They involve a question of art, of the right of the artist to the free choice and treatment of his materials, and the extent to which his freedom of choice and treatment can or should be limited by prudence. They also involve the attempt to limit this freedom by appeals to mass emotion, and by consequent mass pressure. The end result, in each case, has been a semi-ecclesiastical McCarthyism, accompanied by some of the odious methods which this now implies: its "guilt by association," its appeal to prejudice and non-intelligence, its hysteria. This has made the matter of art and prudence a question for debate in the marketplace, and it has called into the debate thousands of well-meaning but misguided voices that appear to know little of the profound meaning of that which they so noisily argue about. It is a spectacle which many of us, as Catholics, can view only with shame and repulsion, for we know that neither art nor prudence, religion nor country, intelligence nor morality can be served by such means. . . .

It seems that the Church, above all other institutions, since she is the very incarnation of Truth, is the one from which, even in her temporal aspects, the spectre of McCarthyism should be most conspicuously absent. For here this spectre of irresponsible disregard for complexity, this use of "labels," this conscious appeal to surface virtue, this exploitation of non-intelligence, must appear much more deplorable than on any Senate floor — *corruptio optimi pessima*. It is to the Church, as to no human society, that we should be able to look for a deep respect for art as well as for prudence. This respect must result in a reverence for art and the artist which will make any interference with that freedom slow, very slow, to come. If it must come (and there are indeed times when it must) it will be only when a truly grave threat to faith or morals exists in the community. And when it comes it will come prayerfully and quietly. Above all it will avoid arbitrary and hasty judgments on the artist; it will scrupulously avoid making art a matter for partisan debate; it will be the last to uphold, tolerate, or advocate a police censorship of the artist, a censorship which knows practically nothing of the profound nature of that on which it passes judgment, a censorship which carries within it the most serious dangers to the dignity of the human spirit and intelligence, to freedom and art. To support an over eager censorship exhibits an unconcern for the hierarchy of values; a profoundly Philistine and un-Catholic brand of arbitrary moralism.

We have the Catholic War Veterans, organized, it would seem, to bear loud witness to those aspects of popular American Catholicism which are most shocking to any mature view of the function of the Church in modern society. Is it not well past the time when a national association of Catholics, especially those who write or teach, should be formed for the purpose of publicly representing and influencing a more reasoned and mature Catholic attitude toward matters on which they could speak with some competence, matters affecting questions of art, education, and the structure of society? Is it not time we cease leaving the field open to those who, however pure and sincere their intentions, seem bent on proving that, perhaps, the Paul Blanshards* of America may have something to say after all?

Has history taught us nothing?

*Paul Blanshard (1892–1980), editor, columnist, attorney, administrator, and author, known for his anti-Catholic views. Among his books are: *American Freedom and Catholic Power, The Irish and Catholic Power,* and *God and Man in Washington.* Ed.

The "Liberal Catholic"

━━ There is a special burden, and the danger of a special presumption, in writing on the concept of a "liberal Catholic." The special burden is the deep historical antipathy which these two words have acquired toward each other, and the consequent difficulty of effecting any reconciliation between them. The danger of presumption lies in seeming to set up a kind of pseudo elite within the Church. "Liberal Catholic" may sound as insufferably smug as "Catholic Intellectual."

Yet the term *is* widely used to describe a type of Catholic whose world view is marked by an enthusiastic acceptance of certain ideals for which liberalism has waged its great battles — maximum human freedom under law, social progress, and democratic equality. And there can be no doubt that the Catholics so described do constitute, if not an elite, at least a definite minority within the Church. The problem then presents itself of whether or not the point of view described in any sense compromises their Christian vocation.

The antipathy which the Catholic and the liberal have felt for each other is real, and its causes are basic to the philosophy of each. When Pius IX solemnly condemned "Liberalism" and denied that the Church could, or should, reconcile itself with "Progress" he pronounced the Church's judgment, once and for all, on that doctrinaire rationalism, secularism, and anti-

Commonweal, 11 July 1952; reprinted, 30 October 1959

clericalism which lay at the base of liberalism's spirit in the nineteenth century. This condemnation was secretly welcomed by many Continental liberals. They heard in it the death knell of the Catholic Church. The condemnation still stands, and the thoroughgoing liberal still reads it as the self-written epitaph of a religion which has announced its removal from the modern world.

As a result of this, the Catholic who associates himself with some of the struggles which are properly identified as "liberal," and who, consequently gains a reputation as a *liberal* Catholic, is apt to find himself suspect among large numbers of his co-religionists. For them, the idea of a Catholic allying himself in any cause with the traditional enemies of the Church suggests a Catholic whose orthodoxy is at best doubtful, and whose loyalty is obviously weak. Certain Catholic journalists spend a lot of their time damning the "liberals," and when they find a "liberal Catholic" they feel sure that they've found a "so-called" Catholic.

But if a "liberal Catholic" is often viewed with suspicion by some of his fellow Catholics, his lot is even less happy among the liberals. The professional liberal is, of course, glad to find an occasional ally among the orthodox, but he is also surprised — and he is skeptical. To the extent that he trusts the man's liberalism, he tends to doubt his genuine Catholicism. Or if he is convinced of this, he begins to doubt his liberalism.

The beleaguered "liberal Catholic" thus stands between two worlds which view each other with mutual distrust, and which, according to their proper lights, exclude each other. Those whose theology he shares frequently distrust him because of his politics, and those with whom he feels at home politically may doubt him because of his theology.

The difficulty is partly a semantic one. Probably no Catholic who bears a reputation for "liberalism" welcomes the "liberal

Catholic" label. The term itself is so burdened with historical and philosophical ambiguities that the kind of all-around misunderstanding described above follows almost inevitably upon its use. It defines nothing and describes only by accident a world view far different from the vague attempts toward religious-philosophical syncretism which it is often interpreted as representing. It is essentially a Catholic affirmation of value wherever value is to be found, and an attempt to recover for the Catholic tradition elements which, through default, have been appropriated by movements hostile to the religious spirit. The "liberal Catholic" is a "liberal" only through the accident of liberalism's having struggled for some things which should properly have a Christian name. His efforts are aimed not at compromise but at recovery and redemption.

It is ironic that although many nineteenth-century liberals actually welcomed the Church's strictures on the modern world, the final victory has belonged to Pius after all. The very things for which he condemned "Liberalism" and "Progress" in the nineteenth century are also the things which have led to liberalism's bad name in the twentieth. Its belief in the inevitability of progress, its overly optimistic estimate of human nature and consequent denial of evil, its dogmatic rationalism — these are ideas turned bitter in the terrible fulfillment of contemporary history. Pius IX would find unexpected allies in 1952. The "liberals" have become the scapegoats for history's failure, and their retreat from their easy hope is in full force. The nineteenth century's hero may well become the twentieth century's forgotten man. It appears more and more fashionable to talk about the future in terms of the "war between the absolutes" — a war in which the well-meaning liberal will find it difficult to take his place.

It would surely have been too much to expect that Catholics would omit taking a certain public satisfaction in this. Unfortunately, that satisfaction has sometimes been almost as indecent as it is presumptuous. All the "we've-always-told-you-so" talk about the "failure of the liberals," and the present low estate of liberalism, seems an extension of something that has been tragically with so much Catholic thinking on the liberal problem for the past one hundred and fifty years. Faced with the very unliberal absolutism on the left, we may have cause bitterly to regret our writing an over hasty obituary to the idealistic liberalism of the center. Because, if the West is to survive the onslaught of the new absolutism of the East, it will only by preserving and revivifying, not the philosophy, but many of the values for which liberalism has fought, almost unaided, in the shaping of the world.

History has already vindicated the Church's condemnation of "Liberalism," and the vindication may well become increasingly complete. Moral relativism, antiintellectualism, Rousseauistic optimism, religious indifferentism — all these by-words of historical liberalism have helped to lead us to the precipice on which we now stand. The tragedy of modern history, then, is not the condemnation itself, but rather what so many liberals — and Catholics — have made of the condemnation.

The liberals have taken the condemnation not only as a rebuke to their philosophy itself, but as a Catholic repudiation of everything for which they have struggled. The Church thus becomes in their eyes not only the enemy of moral relativism, religious indifferentism, and dogmatic rationalism, it also becomes the enemy of political liberty, social equality, and material progress. It becomes the eternal protector of the status quo, the perpetual tender of inquisitional fires, the vigilant enemy of the city of man. And so the fight for the goals of the city of man — for civil freedom, for social and economic equality, for a pluralistic society, assumes the guise of a struggle against the Church.

The liberals have been assisted toward this interpretation by a good many Catholics who, in their reactions against the philosophical errors condemned by the popes, have tended to identify themselves with reactionary political regimes and social philosophies. Their abhorrence of the antireligious spirit which poisoned, and unfortunately continues to poison, so much of the liberal outlook has blinded them to the genuinely spiritual and humanitarian values for which liberalism has fought. The result of this double misunderstanding has been the paradox of liberalism's frequently fighting the right battles for the wrong reasons, and Catholics reacting by fighting the wrong battles for the right reason.

The Church condemned a philosophy of "Liberalism." By extending this to a blanket condemnation of liberals and everything for which they stand, Catholics condemn much that is properly their own, and in reaction espouse things which should be as repugnant to the Christian as they are to the liberal himself.

The outlook frequently described as that of the "liberal Catholic" believes that one of the greatest hopes for the future lies in the recovery and restoration to a Christian context of all things valuable and true. This does not imply any compromise of the faith, any trafficking with the theological enemy. It does imply, however, that on many questions of political and social order the individual Catholic may find himself more in sympathy with the viewpoint commonly associated with liberalism than with the sterile reaction to liberalism common among many of his fellow Catholics. Hence the "liberal Catholic" category to which he is frequently assigned. But he should not be afraid of labels, even though he may regret the fact that they are usually misleading and meaningless.

What is called "liberal Catholicism" is for the most part an attempt to work toward a new synthesis of the Church's unchanging truths with whatever good is to be found in the modern city of man. The "liberal Catholic" is, in the best instances, the twentieth-century Catholic synthesist. He remembers the admonition of St. Paul: "And now, brethren, all that rings true, all that commands reverence, all that makes for right, all that is pure, all that is lovely, all that is gracious in the telling; virtue and merit, wherever virtue and merit are found — let this be the argument of your thoughts."

It has been the high mission of liberalism to fight for much of what is right and true in the modern world, while those who should have aided, and even anticipated its battle, have stood aside, busy reviling "Liberalism" for its philosophical errors, and defending impossibly archaic political and social orders as a bulwark against its aberrations. "Liberalism," as its enemies point out, has indeed failed, and the future of our society will not be the easy utopia envisioned by its nineteenth-century prophets. But its failure has been as a philosophy, not as a vision, and although the future may not lie in the liberal dream, any attempt to build a civilization from which the best elements of that dream are absent is foredoomed to failure. Unless Catholics become more and more aware of this, the phenomenon which Pius XI described as the tragedy of the nineteenth century may be repeated, and this time on an even more catastrophic scale. The Church may now lose not merely a class but a whole world-in-the-making.

What the "liberal Catholic" pleads for is that Catholics should become as passionately dedicated to human dignity and freedom as the liberal has been. Liberalism may have fought its battles for the wrong reasons. The Catholic's mission should therefore be to redeem its struggle by supplying the right ones. The liberal may have advocated freedom of religion and the separation of civil and religious power because he is indifferent to absolute truth. Catholics should join him in advocating the same things because they insist on the absolute inviolability of the human conscience and the freedom of the act of faith. For the same reason they should share the liberal's aversion to censorship, suppression, and the arbitrary uses of temporal power in any effort to coerce the mind of man. History, as well as philosophy, should make them share the liberal's distaste for "calling the cops."

Unfortunately, tragically, the large implications of the lessons in political freedom and social equality which liberalism has taught the modern world have yet to be completely absorbed into popular Catholic thinking. The "liberals" are not always the villains in the denouement of modern culture. Those Catholics who have neglected that part of their Christian heritage which emphasizes human freedom and dignity, and who thus contributed to modern man's alienation from the church, have also played their part. Their zeal to "protect" in a world where a narrow protection is no longer possible, their adamant refusal to repudiate any claim to special privilege in a pluralistic society, their slowness to realize the impossibilities of carrying over methods of public coercion which may have had some justification in a united, sacral order, but which can only cause division and scandal in the modern lay state — all these are things which demand revaluation among Catholics.

This revaluation demands no sacrifice of whatever is essential to the faith; it implies no surrender to relativism or secularism. Rather, it emphasizes the Church's genius for eternal renewal. In order to build what is essential so that the Church may fulfill its mission in the modern world, there must exist a certain willingness to discard whatever of nonessential method and outlook has been carried over from a society which can never return. It is this affirmation, and this revaluation, always in the light of Catholic truth and subject to the guidance of the teaching Church, which the "liberal Catholic" asks of his fellow Catholics in the modern world.

What he earnestly seeks is an increasing Christian charity and (in all which is nonessential) an abandonment of label-thinking. The world is not divided into the "liberals" and the orthodox, the bad guys and the good guys. Men of good will, and vision, and wisdom are not confined to "our" side. The "liberal Catholic," therefore, finally asks that the "liberal" label be dropped in the too easy categorizing of his quest. He would be more content to be thought of as a Catholic who tries to be *catholic*.

The Assault on Culture

— A number of influential European publications, as ideologically diverse as the British Socialist *New Statesman and Nation* and the French Catholic *Esprit,* have deplored the cultural "reign of terror" which they believe exists in the United States. In this they have been joined by some influential Americans, most recently by James Thurber and Arthur Miller. These two artists, writing in the New York *Times,* have expressed deep and angry concern lest that "climate of fear" they see threatening America should stifle the nation's native genius: the willingness to risk; to be bold, unorthodox, and, if necessary, unpopular in intellectual and artistic experiment.

These fears for the continued vitality and independence of American culture have, in spite of the frequency of their expression, remained largely minority fears. The majority of Americans, even those who, like ourselves, are unalterably opposed to the methods of the junior senator from Wisconsin [Joseph McCarthy] have been unable to take seriously the more extreme charges of either the foreign or domestic Cassandras. The contradictory evidence has seemed both too immediate and too strong.

The very fact, for example, that even the most violent of castigations of the United States as a crypto-fascist force in the postwar world have received, and continue to receive, a wide, free, and sometimes enthusiastic hearing in America, has seemed in itself a sufficiently strong rebuke to strictures against the climate of our culture.

The ancient laws of action and reaction work in the area of ideas as well as the realm of physics, and so, it has seemed, the minority hysteria of McCarthyism on the right has produced a counterhysteria on the left. As a result, for those who see a Communist in every liberal there are others who see a fascist in every conservative. The visions of each appear to most responsible Americans about equally myopic, and they have rejected both.

But a rejection of twin hysterias holds its own dangers. The middle way in the matter of cultural freedom in American society must not be trapped into its own special complacency, a complacency which would probably constitute a graver danger to the future of American institutions than the threat of either the right or the left extremists.

For in spite of the excesses of the professional patriots, there does exist a real problem of subversion in the United States, of which the great middle of responsible, unhysterical citizens must be aware. And despite the blindness of unreconstructed "liberals" there does loom on the horizon a cloud of native fascism which, if it continues to move closer, may well become the deadly threat which many feel is already upon us.

The difficult task of preserving the nation's cultural climate thus rests with those citizens who can maintain a sense of critical sanity during a time of great trial and, rejecting the fears and false dichotomies of extremists, will attack those threats to America's freedom which extremists represent.

This may not prove a particularly spectacular nor even notably grateful role. It may well call down the charges of both "fellow traveler" and "red-baiter" upon one who plays it.

The "danger to American culture" may rest not so much in

the hysterias of the extreme right or the extreme left, in themselves (because each extreme is a minority in our land), as in a danger that the healthy center of American opinion will remain complacent, intimidated, or unaware, and thus allow to be lost through default what could never go in conscious struggle.

Informed opinion in the United States must be loud in its continuous insistence on the basically pluralistic structure of our society, and hence quick to defend those accused of "subversion" merely because of their failure to conform to majority patterns of thought or behavior. It must encourage the growth of variety and nonconformity in our cultural patterns, because these are essential to a free society. It must, in short, give the lie to both McCarthyism and a naive liberalism. To the threat of both it must reaffirm America.

"Liberal" vs. "Conservative"

■ Through no choice of its own, *The Commonweal* frequently finds itself described by both its friends and its critics as a "liberal Catholic" publication. The magazine's friends usually mean something quite different in their use of this term than do the magazine's critics, of course, and this fact reinforces the impression that "liberal Catholic" is at best ambiguous and at worst deceptive.

In challenge to that point of view, and in defense of a "rightist" Catholic position, Mr. Frederick Wilhelmsen has written "The Conservative Catholic," an article which seems a significant statement of a position which *The Commonweal*'s editors cannot share.

Hilaire Belloc's dictum, "The Faith is Europe and Europe is the Faith," is a brilliant summary of the attitude which lies behind much "conservative Catholic" thought. It certainly seems to be an attitude implicit in Mr. Wilhelmsen's thesis. But, brilliant or not, Belloc's aphorism expresses a tragically parochial vision of history and religion. For to make an absolute identification of Christianity with "Christendom," no matter how appealing the civilization of Christendom may seem in retrospect, is to formulate a doctrine whose application could mean only atrophy for the Church in the modern world.

It was such a doctrine which led Catholics in France to fight the Republic for a hundred years, making the restoration of the *ancien régime* a cause synonymous with the cause of the Church. Leo XIII eventually rebuked them, of course, reminding them that the cause of the Church is bound to the cause of no particular civilization or political order, but by the time of his rebuke the "tragedy of the nineteenth century" had already occurred.

Even after Leo spoke, however, there were Catholics who thought that he had succumbed to dangerous "liberal" thoughts. They continued to nourish their hatred of the democratic spirit, and they have their heirs today — Catholics who will still admit no good in, or compromise with, the Revolution. They thus place themselves outside of history — a heroic action, perhaps, but one which leaves them no hope of influencing history's course.

We wonder what the "conservative Catholic" of Mr. Wilhelmsen's persuasion would actually have us do. What program of practical action would follow from the application of his philosophy?

We are afraid that, practically applied, the philosophy of the "conservative Catholic" would commit us to such "causes" as the restoration of Otto von Hapsburg and the Holy Roman Empire. We think it would require our support of majoritarian Catholicism, with all in the way of coercion, censorship, and suppression which this implies. We suspect that it would demand our sharing the antimodern attitudes of a Cardinal Segura.* We fear, in short, that it would require us to abandon the twentieth century.

The "liberal Catholic" admits neither the possibility nor the desirability of such an abandonment. He believes that in the

---

*Cardinal Pedro Segura y Sáenz (1880–1957), archbishop of Toledo and of Seville, was expelled from Spain in 1931 by the Republicans but was readmitted and appointed to Seville in 1937. He opposed the Fallange and feared the growth of Protestantism in Spain. Ed.

present "absence of angels" and utopias from this world, both the Church and the individual Catholic must be content to work with men and in the necessarily imperfect civilization of men. He believes that to identify the Church with a romantic past, even a Christian past, is to betray both the Church and the future. He believes that not only the Middle Ages, but also the Renaissance, the Enlightenment, and modern revolutions have taught the world some lessons which all Catholics would do well to learn. He believes that we must live in the modern world, and that it is this world which we must save, for, he reminds his "conservative" friends, we can have no other.

Catholicism in America

■ To begin a discussion of Catholicism in America with the announced aim of being critical and objective suggests the danger of various misunderstandings. Non-Catholics may see in it an attempt to "Americanize" the Church by watering down its dogmas to make them more palatable to "liberal" tastes. Catholics may fear that the ghosts of Modernism, thoroughly exorcised by Pius X, may loom again in such a topic. It might be well, then, to lessen the danger by indicating at the outset the limits of the discussion. They are implied in a famous observation by Cardinal Gibbons: "The American Church must of its very nature be the same as in Rome or Jerusalem; but in the same manner in which its garb takes on the color of its surroundings, it must also be American."

For a Catholic to discuss "Catholicism in America" is therefore not to discuss Catholicism *as such*. The very nature of the Church, as it understands itself and is understood by its members, makes such a discussion impossible to attempt. The Church, in its dogma and sacraments, essentially transcends both time and place. It knows as little of time and place as it knows of Jew and Gentile, freeman or slave. It knows only Christ and his revelation—the same yesterday, today, and forever.

But the Church is not only essentially transcendent; it is also, through its members, incarnate in a given time and place.

Through its members, it affects a culture and is affected, for better or for worse, by the local conditions and challenges which its members meet. In this sense it assumes that "garb" of which Gibbons spoke, and in this sense we can distinguish "Catholicism" in France, in Ireland, in Italy — and in America. Distinguishing, we can see that differences in attitude and behavior, sometimes minor, sometimes important, exist between the Catholic climate in various times and places. To examine the climate of Catholic opinion and attitudes in American culture, its strength and its weaknesses, is the purpose of this article and of those which will follow it in *The Commonweal* during the coming months.

Such a discussion does not seem to be a gratuitous undertaking. Recent controversies have made it increasingly necessary. It may be true that it is only the extremists among both Catholics and non-Catholics whose public statements, books, and magazines have excited current suspicions, but, extremists aside, there are still real problems to be faced. Many non-Catholics, men of goodwill, are sincerely disturbed by what they see as a threat to democratic values from a Catholic minority, and many Catholics, also men of goodwill, are troubled by the threat to spiritual values which the challenge of liberal secularism offers.

To pretend that the fears on either side are completely without foundation in fact, that no ambiguities exist in the present situation, seems to me singularly unreal. And to leave the discussion to Mr. Paul Blanshard* on the one side and to his Catholic counterparts on the other seems to me singularly unwise.

The problem of Catholicism in America, as seen in its extreme form, might be stated as follows: Catholics see the Church as the only force left strong enough to combat an increasingly arrogant secularist invasion of culture. On every side they see

*See note on p. 5. Ed.

challenged those spiritual values without which civilization becomes mere organized barbarism: in education, in the arts, in
entertainment, in politics, in every major sphere of public and
private life neo-paganism, frequently masquerading under the
name of "liberalism" and "freedom," threatens the foundations
of morality, truth, decency, and public order. To preserve not
only the values proper to their own religion but even those basic
to the natural law itself, they must oppose the extension of
secularism under the name of "democracy."

Many non-Catholics, on the other hand, complain that for
all their pious protestations of loyalty to "the American way
of life" Catholics in this country constantly exhibit their contempt for ordinary democratic procedures. They say that through
their organizations, their political influence, and their pressure
groups, Catholics everywhere seek to impose their own minority
will upon the majority — and that they frequently succeed. Believing that Catholics are authoritarian and antiliberal by nature, they fear that eventual Catholic dominance in American
culture would mark the end of free society as we have known it.

Unfortunately, these conflicting fears even in this extreme
form can easily find evidence to support them. By reading various manifestos of American "liberalism" (some issued from high,
ivy-covered places) the Catholic can find strong confirmation
of his fears of doctrinaire democracy. And a weekly examination of certain sections of the Catholic press could keep Mr. [Paul]
Blanshard busy and prosperous for many years to come. Let
us face it. There is a type of monolithic "democracy" being
preached in the United States to which no Catholic could ever
subscribe. And some Catholics draw politically and culturally
authoritarian implications from their faith which free men necessarily find abhorrent. Interestingly enough, the roots of both
these attitudes can be found, I believe, in a common ground.
Strikingly dissimilar at first glance, they seem to be, on exami-

On the first plane, the spiritual, Maritain reminds us, our action must be that of Christians *as such,* for this is the plane of the Church, of her dogma and sacraments. Here, therefore, Catholics must act together.

The same may be said for the activity of Catholics on the third, the "mixed" plane, where the spiritual becomes directly involved with the temporal. Here the higher good, the spiritual, must always be the determining object of the Christian's action. In such situations (one thinks of marriage, education, etc.) where a real conflict might occur between the claims of the spiritual and of the temporal goods, the Christian's obligation is obvious.

On the second plane, however, that of the temporal, the city of man, our action cannot be that of Christians *as such* but only that of Christian citizens of the earthly city. For here the determining object of action is not, properly, eternal life but rather the temporal good of the city. And, for that reason, the rule for action here must ordinarily be not unity but diversity.

For Christians to seek a false unity in the order of the temporal action would be, as Maritain pointed out, contrary to the very nature of things, a dangerous "political materialization of religious energies." And, although Catholics should take positions on temporal matters "in the light and illumination of their Catholic conscience," it would be intolerable if in so doing they should "claim to speak in the name of Catholicism and implied that all Catholics as such should follow their road."

As Maritain concluded, there is indeed a judgment of Catholicism on political and cultural questions, but "this judgment only bears on certain principles seen from a very lofty angle, on which these questions depend, or on certain spiritual values which they imply." It will not tell the individual Catholic what attitude he should take up on most of the specific temporal questions — political, educational, cultural — with which he will be concerned during his lifetime. There is not, nor can there be, a "Catholic" attitude on these. There is only the attitude of the particular Catholic.

The American environment is the heir, par excellence, of those dreams of material progress, human perfectability and an earthly utopia which bemused the genius of Europe during most of the eighteenth and nineteenth centuries. It is a culture which, perhaps more than any other in history, has sought to canonize the temporal. Having escaped the tragedies which awakened Europe from the Enlightenment's dream, America continues to enjoy that dream. In this sense, the most "progressive" of countries is an anachronism in the modern world.

The major modern spokesmen for a materialistic utopia have been the liberal prophets. Through the Enlightenment's "reason" and its weapon, scientism, they have hoped to make the world over in their own image. Their vision has been that of an earthly paradise, and they have sought to include within that vision the totality of human experience.

It is a vision which religious men continue to find not only inadequate and naive, but basically terrifying. They are convinced (and modern history fortifies their conviction) that it is a vision which, rejecting absolute morality, must ultimately result in rejecting man himself. They fear that any abandonment of absolute spiritual values for the sake of a material "progress" is more likely to end in Hitler's jungle than in Rousseau's garden.

It has been remarked that the tyranny of a democratic majority is the most terrible of all tyrannies — "The absolute ruler may be a Nero, but he is sometimes Titus or Marcus Aurelius; the people is often Nero, and never Marcus Aurelius" — and this may be true. Yet, even a majority tyranny, if the majority subscribe to some absolute standard of morality, will be somehow limited and humanized. The tyranny of a majority which rejects all absolute morality, however, is a refinement in horror which it has taken the modern world to discover. It is this horror which the democratic absolutists seem to offer in the name of enlightenment, and it is against this threat that religious men react.

The difficulty is that their reaction to the threat and the slogans of doctrinaire secularism sometimes becomes an equally doctrinaire, equally totalitarian spiritualism. Their challenge to those who distrust the rights of the eternal is to counterchallenge the rights of the temporal. In such a climate, genuine values, both temporal and eternal, are the victims.

I think that the growth of such a climate is the basic problem of "Catholicism in America" today. As the American environment grows increasingly secularized — in education, in literature, in the popular arts and entertainments — Catholics grow more fearful for the survival of spiritual values. And as they do, they attempt to impose a unity and authority on areas of life in which they can make no legitimate spiritual demands. It is a vicious circle. The secularists provide the religious integralists with ammunition to be used against the claims of the temporal, and the integralists, in their turn, give the secularists ammunition for use against the rights of the spiritual. Mr. Blanshard and certain spokesmen for an "integral," "militant" Catholicism really owe each other much.

It would not seem especially appropriate for a Catholic to advise his non-Catholic fellow citizens on what they should do about the threat he sees from their quarter. For one thing, there is probably little he can do about their problem directly. He can merely point it out and warn against it. His hope will be that they will themselves see that the monolith of democratic absolutism is at least as terrifying a threat to free men as any which may come from Catholics — more terrifying, indeed, because it is more immediate.

But it might be appropriate for a Catholic to recommend to his fellow Catholics meditation on a passage from Lord Acton:

"In politics as in science the Church need not seek her own ends. She will obtain them if she encourages the pursuit of the ends of science, which are truth, and of the State, which are liberty." One of the great needs in the American Catholic climate is, I believe, an increased respect for the truth in Acton's observation, which is, ultimately, the truth of Maritain's distinctions on the action proper to Christians on the temporal plane.

For Catholics in America do not lack a zeal for the spiritual. They are orthodox; their churches are full; they seem, on the whole, united and loyal in those things which pertain to eternal life. And on the "mixed" plane of action they seem mature too. Against the threat of secularism they have maintained, sometimes heroically, the sanctity of Christian marriage and the integrity of Christian education. But, on the temporal level, they seem sometimes dangerously unaware. In politics, in literature, in science, and in art, they seem strangely unwilling to render the temporal what is its due, to grant that measure of diversity and freedom which is proper to it.

Absolutisms cannot be transferred from the spiritual to the temporal sphere without doing violence to both spiritual and temporal values. There is a realm of human behavior (that in which most of us operate, practically, all our lives) where an enlightened pragmatism and a respect for tentative judgments are the essential methods of free men. No "Catholic" position is possible here. If Catholics in America can learn a more profound respect for the rights of the temporal, and non-Catholic liberals a more basic reverence for the rights of the spiritual, there need be no further threat to democracy or religion from either side. The obligation involved seems to me to be mutual.

The Area of Catholic Freedom

■ A Catholic, by the profession of his faith, has the advantage of possessing a large area of certain knowledge — the area of those first truths on which the Church has spoken with authority. Here the Catholic is relieved of questions; he has only facts: *Roma locuta est; causa finita est.*

Rome does not speak often, but she speaks clearly and magisterially at those times in history when great issues are in doubt, when the human spirit is assaulted, when she herself must choose between divergent paths. At such a time the Church looks to herself, to her own nature and destiny, and gives final answers. Much of the nineteenth century was such a time. During the pontificate of Pius IX the spirit born of the Enlightenment and revolution reached its full strength and, under the name of progress, threatened the very existence of the Church. Pius IX responded by condemning wholesale those principles and slogans most valued by the Enlightenment and revolution. He denied that the Church could or should reconcile herself with such liberalism or progress as they represented.

There were Catholics who had hoped for a different resolution of the conflict between the Church and modern civilization. Newman and Acton in England, Lacordaire and Dupanloup in France — the great liberal Catholics of the nineteenth century — had sought to avert so decisive a break between the City of God and the City of Man. They had worked for a greater restraint on the part of men in both camps. But this was not a time of restraint, and the moderates lost. The rupture between the Church and the world seemed complete.

But was it complete? Ninety years after Pio Nono's famous Syllabus it seems less so. What perhaps could not be recognized in the hot atmosphere of 1864 seems true now: the work of Pius IX in the area of the Church's relation to modern culture was essentially negative. This is not to deny its necessity or its value. It had to be done. With Italian armies beating against the gates of Rome the Pope could not linger over nice distinctions between what was totally unacceptable and what was redeemable in the spirit of the Risorgimento. What Pius IX named was a spirit the Church could *not* reconcile with her own spirit. He did not attempt to explore—nor, probably, to understand—what the Church could accept in the modern world.

Those Catholics who did attempt this during Pio Nono's reign were destined to frustration and defeat. They lived too soon. But the questions they raised have still to be answered. Lord Acton's writings are relevant today. The basic facts of the Church's unalterable opposition to materialism and relativism were settled in the nineteenth century; the more complex issues of the practical relationship between Catholicism and modern culture are still unresolved. Paradoxically, their resolution should be more possible because of the reigns of Pius IX and Saint Pius X. The dangers of theological liberalism and modernism have been made clear. The limits of orthodoxy have been drawn. No informed Catholic should fall into errors against which he has been so forcefully warned. We should therefore be able to consider things more calmly and more safely than was possible before the Syllabus and the encyclical *Pascendi*.

What are the things we have to consider? What are the unresolved issues which hang over from the great conflicts of the nineteenth century? They seem to me to fall roughly into the general questions of the areas of freedom possible within the Church, the relation of Catholics to the political life of their time, and the attitude to be taken by Catholics toward modern culture. In each of these questions we know what is *not* possible. We are plagued, however, by ambiguous attitudes toward what *is* possible. Here we must still explore and discover, for the sake of both the Church and the world.

And here we can expect no syllabus to show us the way. These are areas primarily of attitude rather than of definition — areas in which no easy guideposts are possible. There are Catholics who think that the important questions have all been solved, that we need only consult the manuals to discover the answers. They would bind us in a nineteenth-century straightjacket as we attempt to grapple with twentieth-century complexities.

Such an attitude is as impossible as it is imprudent. Contingent problems cannot be solved in advance of their appearance. Each generation must face the problems of its own age. It should be guided, of course, by the experience of previous generations, but should not be deceived into thinking that the two experiences are the same. Many of the problems a Catholic must face in 1954 are radically different from the ones Pius IX answered in 1864. We have, as Catholics throughout history have had, a unique present with which to deal.

The situation, for example, which faces Catholics in the United States cannot be met by an appeal to the Syllabus. This country has known none of the fierce antireligious, anticlerical tradition of European democracy. Our institutions were developed in a spirit of respect for religious values. Liberalism and progress never meant in America what they meant to Pius IX when he condemned them. In all this the United States and the Church have been especially favored. What was impossible in nineteenth-century Europe because of the antireligious bias of the age might therefore be possible here.

There is another reason why the United States offers an especially opportune climate for the working out of tensions between the Catholic spirit and modern culture. The Church itself is, in this country, vigorous and united. In Europe during the nineteenth century whole classes were lost to Catholicism, and the fight today is to recover them. France, and in some ways Italy, have become mission countries in which the Church must fight a day-to-day struggle against organized forces encroaching upon those rights she still retains. Spain, still Catholic, is an island apart from the modern world, a country divorced by force from the main currents of the time, and thus has little to offer toward the solution of the time's problems. In this country, however, the best in the modern liberal faith and the strongest in the modern liberal faith find themselves together, and in this fact there is reason for hope.

But serious problems also exist and it seems foolish to ignore them. In spite of — perhaps because of — its favorable situation, the Church in the United States is distinguishable by its conservatism in certain key areas of politics and culture. The churches are full; the people are faithful. Why, it seems, should we unsettle this happy state of affairs by brooding on our imperfections? Why should we risk dividing the unity of Catholic opinion in this country by a public display of differences within the Church? Why indeed, except that complacency in the long run can be deadly and the absence of self-criticism may place us in a permanent state of arrested development.

In the meantime American culture grows increasingly secularized and Catholics do little or nothing to halt this because they are, on the whole, cut off from the major cultural developments of their times. It is easy to denounce modern culture for its subjectivism, its materialism, its relativism; it is easy to use the words "liberal" and "progressive" as epithets to hurl at our contemporaries. It is much more difficult, however, to distinguish what is valuable from what is perverse in modern culture, to take hold of it and turn it, wherever possible, from its suicidal ends toward ends compatible with man's nature and destiny. This demands a positive engagement rather than a negative withdrawal. The great challenge facing Catholics today is the challenge of maturity; of facing rather than evading the problems of their age; of saving rather than condemning the world. If this challenge is to be accepted we will have to face the broad questions of Catholic freedom, politics, and culture much more positively than we have in the past.

What is the legitimate area of freedom within the Church? Obviously, it does not extend to dogma, discipline, or the received traditions of Catholic teaching. It does not include what is commonly understood as the Magisterium of the Church. Pope Pius XII has recently warned against the dangers of "lay theology," that is, against a theology developed independently of the Church's tradition and authority. Whatever falls within the area of that authority, he reminds us, is not the laity's to tamper with.

But the Holy Father has warned not only against "lay theology." He has warned also against a too rigid, and hence unhealthy, unanimity of opinion among Catholics on matters which do not fall within the scope of the Church's teaching office and which, of their nature, admit and demand diversity of views even within the Church. It seems that most questions Catholics are practically concerned with in the United States today — questions of the attitude to be taken toward particular political and cultural issues of our time — are included within this area of freedom. And so it would seem that here a healthy pluralism of opinion should be encouraged within the Catholic community, as well as a mutual respect among Catholics who disagree.

But this situation does not always prevail, and to the extent that it does not we have failed the Church by setting her up as that monolith which her enemies consider her to be. To make the Church appear partisan and parochial is to betray the Church's spirit, which is catholic. To fear that Catholic unity cannot admit open discussion and disagreement among Catholics in areas outside the Church's teaching authority is to sell short the vigor of the Church.

In reality, what scandalizes the world and causes fear of the Church is the sight, not of Catholics' disagreeing, but of Catholics in unanimous agreement on everything under the sun. And quite rightly, for such an image is a monstrosity; it should frighten Catholics too. We all know the ancient formula: in essentials unity; in doubtful matters liberty; in all things charity. We have tended, in the face of assault from a hostile world, to emphasize the first clause. Perhaps we should now begin to lay greater stress on the second and third.

Should a layman, for example, be burdened with the charge of "anticlericalism" if he takes public issue with a cleric in some question of temporal affairs, over some political or cultural problem, some legislation, politician, or play? It does not seem that he should, but he frequently is so burdened today if he exercises what at an earlier time in the Church, or in different countries today, would be considered his legitimate freedom of speech within the Church. Again, what causes real scandal in these matters, uniformity or diversity?

No Catholic can be anticlerical, obviously. But there is a sense in which every Catholic should be anti-"clerical." The distinction of the two is a constant necessity for the health of the Church. The one is life, the other death for the Church's welfare. To charge a fellow Catholic with anticlericalism because of his disagree-

ment with a nonessential position held by his fellow Catholics —
whether in politics or in the arts — is in itself a perversion of
clericalism properly understood; it is a manifestation of "clericalism" at its worst.

A first and necessary step toward a Catholicism more able
to enter into and influence the age seems to be, therefore, the
cultivation and encouragement within the Catholic community
itself of a livelier pluralism, a more vigorous diversity, in all
matters nonessential to the faith. And presiding over this freedom, tempering and directing it, there must be a spirit of charity, a reluctance to advance one's own position as *the* Catholic
position at the expense of the orthodoxy of one's opponent.

This spirit is not something that can be accomplished by de-
cree or easily defined. It is an attitude that must be built slowly
along the way, and it is possible for a Catholic only if it is firmly
based on dogma and kept open to the Church's teaching authority. But we must realize that in the Church on earth, as in
the Church in heaven, there are many mansions, and that the
freedom of the sons of God is something wider than those outside the Church can sometimes see or understand.

The temptation which betrays many Catholics into diminishing the area of freedom possible within the Church is the same
one that leads them into an excessive rigidity in political and
cultural affairs. It might be called the "principled" temptation,
and it is based on an error we might characterize as the "essen-
tialist" error.

We are proud of our richness of principle and quick to deplore a lack of principle in our opponents; we are quick to seize
on essences — to get to "the nature of things" — and ever ready
to denounce the superficiality of those whose view of reality
stops at mere externals. But this attitude has its own pitfalls.
We frequently tend to pronounce upon complex realities as if
they were merely principles, merely essences stripped of their

particular existences. It is thus easy, too easy, for us to cate-
gorize reality, to distinguish our "friends" from our "foes," at
one quick glance, and to demand of others conformity to our
own judgment if they are to pass as "right-thinking" citizens.
This is the ancient folly of the *bien pensants.*

Jacques Maritain has written of "the terrible general tendency
of the conservative world to link the defense of its material interests with the defense of religion." This tendency is surely the
danger in a purely "principled" approach to the temporal order —
whether in the area of politics or the arts. We establish something as being, in principle, friendly to religion and, without
further ado, identify the cause of religion with the cause of this
thing. Therefore, if a political party professes a "militant" anti-
communism it deserves our support; if a novel takes an optimistic view of all things Catholic it is good. And the reverse
holds too. If a political party or a novel does not do these things
we denounce them. In all this we are betrayed into slogans and
into a distortion of reality itself which, being complex, demands
a complex judgment.

The great betrayal is to identify the cause of the Church with
what are essentially temporal causes, to bind the Church to
contingent things, to multiply "Catholic" positions without necessity. And, in this country at least, such a multiplication
comes more frequently from quarters which pride themselves
on strict orthodoxy than from those Catholics loosely known
as "liberal." We are thus frequently presented with a "Catholic"
position on every particular problem that arises to vex us — on
every politician, every novel, every play. The admission of Red
China to the United Nations? No Catholic can consider its possibility even in the future. Faulkner's novels? We should ban
them. The Hollywood Production Code? We must fight any effort to change it.

Doubtless, such rigidity is a caricature of the Catholic position. Unfortunately, this caricature is all that many non-Catholics see as they observe some of the more articulate manifestations of Catholicism in America today. This is the problem we must recognize and, to the extent that it exists, change if we are to contribute significantly, as Catholics, toward resolving the larger political and cultural problems of our milieu. We must work toward a Catholic climate which is more open to the problems of the world, and which approaches them in a spirit of humility rather than with an attitude of despair.

Too much of our thinking seems a hangover from the church-state conflicts of the nineteenth century, a purely negative rejection of our age. Indeed, many of us seem determined to add to the Syllabus of Pius IX, to build up our own private appendix to that famous condemnation. It would be better to leave such tasks to the Holy See, which will warn us quickly enough when warnings are needed. In the meantime our work should be the more positive one of building whatever bridges are possible between the Church and the world. And this we can accomplish only through an expansion of freedom, charity, and tolerance for those both within and outside of the Church.

The Lesson of Captain Dreyfus

▬ History has its moments of universality when, through some individual drama, the perennially basic issues of man and society are again brought on the stage for the world to consider and debate. At such moments the important things — the things that determine the course of civilizations and cultures — once more are made clear. And at such moments there is no possibility of indifference: men must choose sides; they must argue and perhaps end by fighting each other. For these are history's moments of transcendence, of grandeur, when pettiness and self-concern are lost in the majesty of some universal cause.

Ironically, such dramas need not — and often enough do not — involve a cast of thousands or even well-known performers. There may be only one or two men whose destiny is at stake, and these men may be obscure or even, in themselves, uninteresting. But this irony adds to the point, which is that the solution to great problems often hinges upon small factors, and that at history's greatest moments the merely individual and the petty are forgotten in a universal concern for larger things.

Certainly in our own country in our own time both the Sacco-Vanzetti case and the McCarthy dispute (in its major aspects) assumed at least the appearance of some universal cause. In both of these controversies the real question at stake was not of individuals as such but of issues fundamental to the procedures

Commonweal, 7 October 1955

of a civilized society—issues of justice and prudence, of Man and the State. And in both of these controversies the nation was bitterly divided along ideological lines, even though many on both sides did not realize this fact at the time.

Those who wept when Sacco and Vanzetti died wept not so much for these poor men as for what they believed was the death of justice in Massachusetts. And in the McCarthy controversy the junior senator from Wisconsin was actually quite unimportant. (Who cared, really, about McCarthy's income tax returns or his manners in debate?) What was important, urgently important, was the problem for which Senator McCarthy served as an uncomprehending symbol—the problem of individual rights versus some form of total security. Joseph R. McCarthy's pathetic function was to make this problem a matter for national argument. He himself probably never realized what the argument was all about.

In this, he had his forbears in history—men whose individual destinies came to determine the course of national destinies without their ever comprehending what was really going on. In the Dreyfus Affair, perhaps the most significant and bitterly argued political-moral drama of modern times, Alfred Dreyfus himself never understood what had aroused the passions of the world and divided men into hostile camps. To him it was merely a question of his military superiors' having been "misinformed," and his only concern was to set the record straight and thus vindicate the honor of the French army as well as his own. When the affair was finally over, after years of the most terrible and universal bitterness, Léon Blum wrote that Dreyfus, had he not been Dreyfus but someone else, would not even have been a Dreyfusard. Late in his life, when someone spoke to Dreyfus about the historic role he had played in focusing the world's attention on fundamental questions of human rights, he protested: "No, no. I was only an artillery officer prevented by a tragic error from following my career. Dreyfus, the figurehead of justice, was not I; he was created by you."

But though Alfred Dreyfus himself could not understand what his case meant — and continues to mean — to civilized society, it is important that the rest of us understand, that we do not forget lessons that were so hardly learned. *Captain Dreyfus: The Story of a Mass Hysteria,* a new book by Nicholas Halasz, provides the occasion for recalling and again rehearsing one of the central problems of modern times — one which has never been finally resolved and one over which we remain divided today. As long as the problem of Man versus the State remains a problem, the Dreyfus Affair, its classic prototype, will remain a current event.

The facts of the Dreyfus Affair can be briefly summarized. Following France's humiliating defeat by Germany in 1870, there was widespread fear of German espionage in French political circles. This fear was fully justified, and in order to save its own skin the French government decided that traitors must be quickly found. In 1894, therefore, on the most flimsy evidence and after a military trial behind closed doors, Alfred Dreyfus, an unknown Jewish officer of the French General Staff, was convicted of espionage for Germany and sentenced to lifelong deportation to Devil's Island. The nation's fears of espionage were thus quieted. The traitor, it was believed, had been found — and he was a Jew, so, people said, one might have expected such a thing all along.

Two years later, in 1896, however, Colonel Picquart, head of the information division of the French General Staff, became convinced, after a careful survey of the evidence, that Dreyfus was innocent and that the real traitor was not a Jew but a French aristocrat, Major Count Walsin-Esterhazy. The colonel quickly informed his superiors of his belief. They were dumbfounded and outraged. Why, they demanded to know, was he concerned about this obscure Jew? After all, they argued, the honor of the

French army and the security of the French state were involved. Both would be undermined if this case were reopened and an admission of error made. Colonel Picquart, therefore, was conveniently removed to a dangerous post in Tunisia.

Picquart's conscience could not be so easily dismissed, however, and he publicized the facts he had discovered. Soon, agitation for reexamination of the evidence was begun. In 1897 Clemenceau began to fight for a revision of the verdict and, soon afterward, Zola published his mighty *J'accuse*.

What happened then is history. Not only France but the whole civilized world became divided into the camps of Dreyfusards and anti-Dreyfusards. In the words of Mr. Halasz:

> So began a morality play that was to achieve a grandeur unparalleled in the history of the modern state and make France examine in fire and in fear the bedrock upon which democracy is founded. The sanctity of the individual, yes. A noble ideal, no doubt. But as a practical matter, should the whole be sacrificed for the minutest part? Is the moral vindication of one Frenchman worth jeopardizing the security of all Frenchmen?
>
> In facing the question France, the nation of reason, went out of her mind. Normal life stopped. Only a handful of men retained faith in the ability of democracy to provide security for all. The rest had faith only in the State and its Army, and went into paroxysms over any act that reflected on it. In the words of a contemporary writer, "Heroism was needed even to utter the word justice. To protest against the violation of right was made out a crime, and to doubt the infallibility of a military court was considered treason."

The Dreyfusards throughout the crisis were a passionate minority. Against them stood masses of French opinion which demanded no sympathy for "traitors" and "death to the Jews." Against them also stood the French state, which was determined that this case must not be reopened — that, whatever mistake had been made, the "honor" of the French army must be preserved from any suggestion of corruption. On the one hand were those who believed that the rights of the individual, even the most obscure individual, are worth more than the prestige of any state; on the other were those who believed that, come what may, the principle of authority must be preserved — and that one individual injustice counts for nothing against the security of an entire nation.

The affair rocked the world for twelve years. After twelve years the Dreyfusards won. Dreyfus was pardoned in 1899 and finally, in July 1906, he was acquitted of all charges by a court of appeals. But in those twelve years, in the words of Mr. Halasz, "the handful of men who fought for the truth and thus for the restoration of the human ideal as a fortress stronger than any army were defamed, cursed, despised, physically attacked, despoiled of their honors, their offices, jailed, driven into exile. . . . In the end they forced their will on a nation that had become an anarchic mob and returned it to the rule of law. But memorable years of horror and grandeur separated them from that consummation."

What was the Dreyfus case fought over? It is clear that, whatever the particular motivation of men on both sides, the real issue which rocked the world in this struggle was the issue of individual justice versus national security, the issue of the rights of the human person versus the demands of authority. This is the issue which gave the case its grandeur, its universality, its eternal relevance.

"What matters this man's fate?" is a question that will always be asked — and it will always receive bitterly opposed answers. In his September 21 [1955] syndicated column "Today in Wash-

ington," for example, David Lawrence suggests that recent Soviet espionage in the United States and in Britain was made
possible, "because the atmosphere was poisoned by the specious
claim that individual rights are sacrosanct — as if any individual rights could ever supersede the right of the state to protect
itself against subversion, sabotage or treason."

Here is the Dreyfus problem again, and it is clear where Mr.
Lawrence stands on it. But there are those who would disagree
with him violently, passionately, to the death, if necessary —
men who would insist that basic human rights may never, must
never, be violated, whatever the excuse; and that the state which
would violate them in the name of "security" or of anything else
is a state not worth preserving. These were the men — Colonel
Picquart, Clemenceau, Zola, Jaurès — who fought for Alfred
Dreyfus as for an abstract principle without which no nation's
life is worth living. And against them stood all who made Authority the cardinal principle of political life.

In her brilliant essay on the Dreyfus Affair in *The Origins
of Totalitarianism*, Hannah Arendt points out that the Dreyfusards succeeded in winning over large sections of all classes to
their cause — except one. "The Catholics," she observes, "reacted
as a bloc; among them there was no divergence of opinion."
The entire French Catholic press led the fight against any re-
opening of the Dreyfus case. And, as Miss Arendt says, even
"more striking . . . than the attitude of the Catholics in France
was the fact that the Catholic press throughout the world was
solidly against Dreyfus." Why this shameful fact? Why were
Catholics alone united in support of the anti-Dreyfusard cause?

The answer seems to lie in the Catholic's terrible temptation
to ignore the structure of individual problems for the sake of
some general principle. Nineteenth-century Catholic opinion
hated what the French Revolution represented. Nineteenth-
century liberals opposed the Church. Dreyfus was defended by

liberal heirs of the Revolution: therefore, Catholics apparently reasoned, Dreyfus *must* be guilty.

As Mr. Halasz puts it, during the Dreyfus Affair "the Catholic press went straight to the heart of the matter. The Great Revolution was described as an insurrection of man against God and was called the original sin of the century." Catholic opinion thus saw the defeat of Dreyfus as a means for avenging itself on the antireligious, liberal world, and it stopped at practically nothing in its attempts to vilify Dreyfus and those who defended him. Catholics somehow equated the guilt of Dreyfus with the guilt of the modern world. By a perversion of logic they seemed to reason that because the modern world was guilty, Dreyfus was guilty. And because Catholics overwhelmingly stood for "authority" against the revolutionary "rights of man" they spared no effort to uphold the authority of the French state against those who they believed would undermine it in this affair.

One French priest put the majority Catholic position forcefully in an address at a college festival at the height of the affair:

When I speak of the necessity of a nation to arm itself with power I mean the material power that does not reason, but imposes itself — the power of which the Army is the most forceful expression, the power of the cannon, which is the ultimate argument of statesmen and of nations. . . . The enemy is intellectualism which professes to disdain power. Turn the point of the sword against it. Woe to the government that veils its weakness behind a supposed insufficiency of legal powers and lets the sword drop. The country in the grip of anxiety will reject those who refuse to save her even at the price of bloodshed.

With the ultimate vindication of Dreyfus the republican-liberal cause was strengthened and the "rights of man" were reestablished as the recognized basis of French law. The authoritarians who had sought to establish their case on the conviction of one man were thus routed. Clemenceau, bitter from the struggle, was determined that never again should clerical influence be felt in the French state, and he caused the violently anticlerical laws of the early twentieth century to be enacted. Those who had made intolerance and injustice part of their cause were rewarded with intolerance and injustice. Thus it always was, and thus it will always be.

But whatever later injustices they perpetrated, much can be forgiven those who fought for this Jewish captain. In the face of national hysteria they achieved a transcendent victory. Heroically, they rescued the impartiality of law from mob passion, and against the massed opposition of prejudice they vindicated the individual's inviolable rights. As one of them, Jean Jaurès, wrote: "What matter the errors of fate and false directions of life? A few luminous and fervent hours are enough to give meaning to a lifetime."

Between Morality and Power

■ This publication is only six months old, but already some of its readers suggest it has taken a stand with the "realists" on the questions of ethics and world affairs. And the final meaning of "realism," they say, is power pure and simple, the sacrifice of principle to expediency, whatever lip service may be paid to virtue along the way to its defeat. This is the argument made in a number of letters we have received, one of which, the communication from Professor William A. Banner of Howard University, is published elsewhere in this issue of *Worldview*.

The argument is a serious one, and *Worldview* takes it seriously. This journal has no interest in allying itself with any particular school of morality, as morality relates to international affairs. Indeed, it thinks that one of its chief functions is to make a continuing examination of all "schools." It hopes to provide a medium for dialogue between men of opposing views — realists and idealists, liberals and conservatives, Protestants and Catholics, Jews. Through dialogue, it hopes at least to indicate what the problems facing our statesmen and our moralists are.

Worldview has no moral programs; it has, rather, moral concerns. Because, it is convinced, the answers we seek (if, in so complex an area as ethics and foreign affairs, we may speak of "answers" at all) lie well beyond the categories of fixed programs or positions. They will be arrived at through wisdom rather than through rules.

For these reasons, among others, this magazine distrusts the single-minded application of any position to current problems. It is worried over the fact that, in an age of unparalleled moral threat, much of our national thinking is postulated solely on considerations of power. It is worried, too, over the fact that in an age of unparalleled physical threat much of our religious thinking is postulated solely on considerations of abstract virtue. Examples of both are easy to come by. An instance of the former is cited in the editorial from *Christianity and Crisis* . . . ; an instance of the latter is seen in some aspects of the foreign policy statement recently issued by the leaders of a major Protestant denomination.

The question of nuclear testing has become, in many quarters, an emotion-charged issue, a shibboleth used to separate the good from the wicked. On the one side, if a man is for "security" he is for continuing the tests; on the other, if a man is for "peace" he is for the immediate cessation. Period. Both sides fail to consider that the question of nuclear testing cannot be decided in a vacuum; it must be judged within the much larger and complex context of peace with justice in our time.

But *Christianity and Crisis* is surely speaking to the point when it deplores the moral complacency over testing that seems implicit in many of our government's official pronouncements. As *Christianity and Crisis* acknowledges, there are many other considerations besides the moral which our government and the churches must take into account. But, when all the considerations are weighed, the moral consideration remains a major one. To ignore it, or to treat it as a luxury this nation cannot afford in time of peril, is to distort reality itself. Yet this is what much of our "official" and our popular thinking seems to do.

History indicates that it takes the popular imagination a generation, at least, or else the shock of direct experience, to adjust to a new reality. This nation went into World War I as though it were going to a picnic. It did not really know what modern warfare means. But it entered World War II grimly: its imagination had been chastened by the horrors of 1918.

There is, alas, little reason to think that this nation now realizes what World War III — a war fought with massive thermonuclear weapons — would mean. We are duly grim about warfare, of course, but ours is the grimness proper to a pre-thermonuclear world. We still tend (on the popular level, at least) to think and to speak of a new world war as a last-resort option. "How dead can you be? after all."

Unfortunately, "you," we, they — all together — can now be deader than was ever possible before in human history. For the first time in human history everyone, everything, can be dead. And this fact gives the moral problem of armaments an urgency, a relevancy, it never had before. To treat power as power pure and simple, divorced from morality, is the ultimate unreality. We live in a world where power and morality are irrevocably joined.

But if our "official" and popular thinking is too much given to moral complacency, some of our religious thinking is too much given to moral abstraction. The recent pronouncement on U.S. foreign policy, issued by a great Protestant denomination, raises some troubling questions for the relationship between ethics and world affairs.

The statement deplores the fact that the United States "counts among its allies some nations which are in no sense free. By our actions we proclaim to the world that lands where human freedom is utterly dead can qualify for membership in the free world simply by supplying military bases or strategic commodities. . . . This kind of international hypocrisy should be abhorrent to Christians."

And addressing itself, apparently, to the question of the summit meeting, the statement proclaims that there can be "no substitute for personal encounter in the pursuit of human understanding. . . . When men who profess the Christian religion make no adequate provision for a face-to-face encounter with their enemies, they betray the religion they profess."

This statement is admirable in its tone of moral integrity. And it does a public service in indicating how unsatisfactory, really, the term "free world" is. Obviously, if this term is interpreted narrowly, it does not describe our present alliances. But then, if we insist on interpreting it narrowly, we are probably not going to have any effective alliance against Soviet aggression at all. In the imperfect world we have to live in, with the ambiguous powers with which we must deal, all that "free world" can possibly mean is "free from Soviet domination." (And surely there can be no nation on earth — even the Soviet Union — where human freedom is "utterly" dead.)

And one must wonder, too, whether it is wise to make a "face-to-face encounter" between the leaders of this nation and their enemies a clear-cut dogma of the Christian faith. One supposes that no Christian, or any other religious man, can be opposed to personal encounter. But one supposes, too, that a good many religious men can think of instances when personal encounter — for any number of reasons — will do more harm than good. Whether any particular kind of encounter is one of those instances is a question to which a responsible morality must address itself.

The point is, of course, that neither power nor morality can speak relevantly to our condition's total context. Abstracted from that context, either may be irresponsible, or dangerous, or, finally, fatal.

Worldview is not concerned either with ethics or with foreign affairs in themselves. It is concerned with seeking some meeting between the two, a meeting that can be brought about within the walls of no single "school." Imperfection is the pathos of politics. Perfectionism is the pathos of morality. Somewhere between the two we find wisdom which, in our time, means finding a new way for the human race to survive, with justice and with peace.

How American Protestantism
Looks to a Roman Catholic

■ If there be *a* Christian commandment, it is surely the commandment of love. "By this," Jesus told us, "will all men know that you are my disciples, if you love one another." But if the standard of this commandment were strictly applied, we would find few "Christians" in any age. As for the situation in America today, Reinhold Niebuhr has accurately observed: "The relations between Catholics and Protestants in this country are a scandal and an offense against Christian charity."

The scandal of our Protestant-Catholic relations may, of course, be inevitable. Only the saints approach the sublimity of Christ's commandment of love. The rest of us are conditioned by our own prejudices, and all of us — Catholics and Protestants — are heirs to a four-hundred-year history of suspicion and, even, dislike. Looking at the relations of Catholics and Protestants in many parts of Europe, however, one would have to be a pessimist indeed to doubt that the situation in the United States could be improved.

I have been asked to contribute a Catholic's — a *particular* Catholic's — view of American Protestantism. In thinking about this, I see again that objectivity comes hard. We are all (I repeat) conditioned by our own prejudices. For most Catholics,

In Wayne H. Cowen, ed., *Facing Protestant-Roman Catholic Tensions* (New York: Association Press, 1960).

Protestantism is a peculiarly inexplicable phenomenon. And though many of my coreligionists may disagree with some things I say in this article, I think they will agree with this: for most Catholics, an ordered skepticism is easier to understand than Protestantism. Obviously this is not an easy or a pleasant fact for a Catholic to admit, especially when he is writing for a primarily Protestant audience. But it is true, and it indicates something profound about Catholic-Protestant difficulties.

James Joyce expressed this classically in a famous passage toward the end of *A Portrait of the Artist as a Young Man*, where Stephen Dedalus (Joyce himself) tells his friend Cranly that he is abandoning Catholicism:

> "Then — said Cranly — you do not intend to become a Protestant?"
>
> "I said that I had lost the faith — Stephen answered — but not that I had lost self respect. What kind of liberation would that be to forsake an absurdity which is logical and coherent and to embrace one which is illogical and incoherent?"

However arrogant this passage may sound to Protestants, I think they should realize that Joyce was here expressing something more profound than Catholic prejudice or Irish insularity. He was stating a conviction almost universally held among Catholics, that there is no alternative to the Church of Rome except disbelief. For most Catholics, Protestantism, with its innumerable divisions, seems at best compromise and at worst chaos. Our own concept of the Church, with its system and logic, its tradition and order, does not prepare us for sympathy with any version of Christianity less "certain" or more ambiguous than our own. We are apt to see in Protestantism a mere shadow-Christianity, the sad example of what happens once the objectivity of Catholic authority is overthrown.

I would not argue here whether this is good or bad, but it

has important consequences for Catholic-Protestant relations on almost every level. Since Catholics tend to see Protestantism as mere negation, mere *anti*-Catholicism, they tend also not to take it seriously as a genuine *Christian* concern, even in the social and political orders. From this fact much of the religious misunderstanding in our pluralist society results.

One outstanding and discouraging fact about the Catholic-Protestant situation in America is that, on the popular level at least, most of our controversies are conducted on the level of caricature. The Protestant caricature of Catholicism is a monolith called "Romanism," which is authoritarianism pure and simple. The Catholic caricature of Protestantism is that mere negation, that compromise-Christianity which it is so easy to dismiss. Because of these caricatures, Protestants approach Catholicism with unreasoning suspicion, and Catholics view Protestantism with fatuous condescension. Thus are the real issues between us evaded.

Both caricatures are obviously sins against charity and truth, and the first object of any Catholic-Protestant encounter should be to destroy them. But before this can be done, each group must admit, quite honestly, its own responsibility for creating and maintaining the caricatures. Catholics must take some of the blame for their own part in maintaining that "monolithic" caricature of the Church which they deplore. And Protestants must acknowledge their responsibility for presenting a spectacle of negativism and anti-Catholicism on the American scene.

I do not believe that Catholics generally have anything that approaches an adequate understanding of what Protestantism actually *is.* Most of them know only what it is *not.* And this is a major failure in Catholic education.

I recall my own education. It was in Catholic schools from the first grade through my master's degree, and I am most grateful for it. But I am not grateful for what it taught me — or, more accurately, for what it failed to teach me — about Protestantism.

In primary and secondary schools I learned the standard things, all negative: Protestants reject the authority of the pope; they do not honor the Virgin Mary; they deny the efficacy of good works; they acknowledge only two sacraments, and so forth. In the college that I attended I learned nothing more. (But the history department offered a two-semester course under the interesting title, "The Protestant Revolt and the Catholic Reformation.") Through eighteen years of Catholic education I heard nothing positive about Protestantism; no teacher ever suggested that, beyond the Reformation's negations, Protestantism has a prophetic vision of its own vocation. (I would note here my suspicion that, in the teaching of Roman Catholicism, Protestant schools do no better.)

If the religious situation in America is to improve, Catholics must understand — better than they have in the past — that Protestantism has its own unique genius, that it witnesses to some of the central truths of Christianity, that, at its best, it is moved by a special sense of God's awful majesty and a special jealousy for his sovereign rights. And Catholics can admit these things even though they must finally judge Protestantism to be separated from the Church's visible unity and doctrinally incomplete.

More than this, a Catholic can be thankful for the witness Protestantism bears to some aspects of Christian truth and the Christian vocation that, at various times in the Roman Church's history, may be obscured. I, for one, am grateful to Methodism for the witness it bears to the life-giving action of the Holy Spirit, and to Presbyterianism for its careful guarding of "the Crown Rights of the Redeemer"; I am grateful to Anglicanism for its deep sense of seemliness and order in worship, to Lutheranism for its emphasis on the grace of God, and to the Congregational churches for their special awareness of the responsibility of the local community of believers in the total life of Christianity. I am grateful to Protestantism generally for its devotion to the prophetic ministry of the church.

God does work in mysterious ways, and the Catholic should see the hand of God in all these things. One of John Henry Newman's most moving letters was that in which he declared, after many years as a Catholic, that he would "never" attack the Anglican church. How, he asked, can any Catholic attack a community in which so much of God's truth is proclaimed and so much evidence of God's grace is to be seen?

The faces of Protestantism in America are more various, probably, than in any other country; the various gifts of Protestantism are consequently more manifest here, too. I hope it will not seem ungracious of me to say that, because of this, Protestantism's special defects are perhaps more evident here than in any other place. What the American Catholic sees when he looks at Protestantism are often, unfortunately, those things about which Protestantism can be least proud: a narrow moralism, anti-Catholicism, and what I would describe as a kind of crypto-Erastianism. (I would be the first to admit that, when he looks at Catholicism in America, the Protestant may well see evidence to confirm *his* worst suspicions of the Church of Rome: clerical paternalism and a philistine antiintellectualism. But this is not the subject of my article.)

Theologically and historically, Protestantism and Catholicism are separated by disagreements that — except for divine intervention — will probably never be healed. There will never be a Protestant Catholic church, nor will there ever be a Catholic Protestant church, at least in any sense that a Roman Catholic could admit. But of all the differences between the two traditions, few are more significant than the primacy each tradition assigns to the intellect and to the will.

The Catholic tradition stands eternally for the primacy of the intellect over the will, of the logos over the ethos; historic Protestantism has tended to be voluntaristic, to give primacy to the will. For a Catholic, goodness is for the sake of truth; for most Protestants, truth is for the sake of goodness. There seems little doubt that the intense moralism of modern Protestantism is a result of this ordering. The Protestant, almost by self-definition, is a "good" man; the Catholic, by self-definition, is a man who holds the truth.

I have no intention of discussing here the merits of either tradition, but both, obviously, have their effects in social and cultural life, and both have their temptations. If the natural temptation for the Catholic — with his assurance of "truth" — is an arrogant dogmatism, the natural temptation for the Protestant — with his concern for "virtue" — is a puritanical moralism. This is the temptation, I believe, to which a good portion of American Protestantism has succumbed, and because our culture is a predominantly Protestant culture, the American ethos has succumbed to it too.

This obviously is not something about which a Catholic has any right to complain. One cannot reasonably "blame" a culture for the way it has developed. What a Catholic does have a right to complain of, however, is the assumption among large numbers of American Protestants that their own version of morality — which a Catholic sees as a sectarian-puritan version — is in some way part of the American-way-of-life. There is a great irony in the fact that those Protestant groups that are most keen on "separation" of the church and state, and most worried about the Catholic "threat" to separation, are also the groups that would impose a Protestant ethos on the community through civil law, wherever possible. The absolute prohibition of drinking and gambling through civil legislation is, of course, the major example of this.

How is this achieved, this identification of a Protestant puritanism with Americanism itself, by men sincerely devoted to
"separation" of church and state? I suspect it is by what I have
called a kind of crypto-Erastianism among many American Protestants. Historically, Protestants have often embraced an Eras-
tian theory of church-state identification. In this country they
are, overwhelmingly, in favor of church-state separation. In
many cases, though, they seem to be in favor of separation as
a weapon against "Rome." They are for separation of the church
from what they still assume to be an implicitly Protestant state.

All this is, of course, on the level of emotion. It would not,
could not, be defended rationally. But I think it is operative —
and significantly operative — nonetheless. On the subconscious
level many Protestants still think of the United States as *their*
country and fight to keep it so. But they do not see this as a
violation of separation: they are fighting to keep America "American," by which they mean Protestant in its predominant mores
and symbols.

I realize that I am here criticizing a phenomenon that is dying.
The most responsible voices in American Protestantism have
for many years been warning against the assumption that Protestantism is somehow *the* American religion and that Catholics
and Jews are not quite in the club. But it takes time for popular sentiment to catch up with intellectual perception, and Catholics of my generation still feel the heavy hand of Protestant "purity" upon us in many areas of American life.

We still feel, too, the sharp cut of anti-Catholicism, even when
it is "civilized," patronizing, and well meant. I would not trouble
the reader by pointing to the more primitive expressions of anti-
Catholicism that still exist in our land and are reflected in some
recent Gallup polls. This does not bother me or, I think, most
Catholics. It is vestigial; it is almost — but not quite — dead. What
does bother me a good deal is the challenge, still given us, to

"prove" our Americanism, and we hear this challenge even at "advanced" interfaith gatherings. I, for one, am very tired of explaining that, no, I *really* feel no conflict between my Americanism and my Catholicism. The day is rapidly coming — I think it has come for me — when American Catholics will refuse to answer such challenges, no matter how well they are meant, and will return them for the insults they are.

What I hope for in American Protestantism is that it continue to move in the direction it is now moving — away from sectarianism, from a narrow moralism and an obsessive anti-Catholicism — toward reemphasis on those things that are great and profound in its own tradition. I hope it will worry less about "Rome" and about such, in my view, inane issues as an ambassador to the Vatican, and more about the real danger it faces in making too cozy an alliance with the forces of American secularism. I hope Protestantism deepens its own best heritage: that its renewed concern for the church and the sacraments, for Christian unity and ecumenical encounter, are the signs of its future. I hope that both Catholics and Protestants will increasingly realize that we have much to learn from each other. Because, though the achievement of Christian unity must wait upon God's good time, we are all, even now, baptized in the same Christ.

A Liberal View

▬ William F. Buckley, Jr., and I have met in debate three times this year. Each time I have heard him describe my own "liberal" Catholic position, and have failed to recognize it. I still await some debate in which he will tell us what a "conservative" Catholic is. Because the "liberal" and "conservative" question is not one defined by the easy labeling and categorizing that are the stock in trade of many magazines — both on the left and on the right. It is a question that cannot be profitably discussed in Mr. Buckley's terms of easy blacks and whites, of "angels" and "devils."

This question of the Catholic in the modern world, of what the attitude of the Catholic should be toward problems of the modern world, is not a simple conservative question of rejecting the modern world or a simple liberal question of embracing the modern world — although, in the course of polemics, the question is sometimes reduced to this. It is not a question of being either "for" the modern world or "against" it. It is rather the complex, serious, and history-laden question of the general *approach* of Catholics to the modern world. It is a question of attitude. And here we must begin by making some basic distinctions.

In the first place, every Catholic — and this includes every "liberal" Catholic — is in a certain sense a conservative. And this is true by definition. It would be monstrous to maintain otherwise. The Catholic accepts a revelation that was once and for all delivered to the apostles; it is part of his patrimony to conserve this revelation and to pass it on.

So the question here of the liberal and the conservative Catholic is not a doctrinal question. Doctrinally, every Catholic is a conservative, and is proud to be a conservative. The notion of a doctrinally liberal Catholicism, if it ever existed, was disposed of once and for all in the condemnations of Pius IX and of Pius X.

The question here then is not doctrinal. It is: given these facts, given these distinctions, what should be the attitude of Catholics toward the modern world? And it is here, in the question of attitude rather than of doctrine, that the terms liberal and conservative assume meaning — at least as descriptions if not as definitions. It is from this standpoint that I wish to consider them.

Now, this question of the approach of the believer to the "modern world" is an ancient question; it is more ancient than the Christian church. This is the question that the psalmist asked in one of the greatest, most moving psalms of the Old Testament. The psalmist asked: "How shall I sing the Lord's song in a strange land?" And believers must repeat the psalmist's question in every age, because in every age there is a conflict between "the world" and the believer. The Prince of this world is at work through history, and any believer who thinks that he serves his faith by subjugating it to the moment, to the demands of the age or to the demands of the century, betrays his faith. The believer is always a stranger and a pilgrim; his question therefore will always be: "How shall I sing the Lord's song in a strange land?"

In seeking to answer this question, the believer faces two obvious temptations. The first temptation is simply to reject the city of man; and this is the temptation to utter transcendence. Certain Christians in every age have succumbed to this temptation. It is a temptation, I think, which historically is more at home with a certain type of Calvinism than it is with Catholicism; but Catholics succumb to it, too. They reject the world as evil; they turn their backs upon it and say: "Here we have our oasis of truth — outside there is the night. Let us build our walls. Let us hold fast to the truth we have. Let us not open the doors." This is the historic temptation of the conservative.

The second temptation comes most easily to certain forms of liberal Christianity, and finds its ultimate expression, I suppose, in such a form of liberal Christianity as Unitarianism; and that is the temptation simply to embrace the "modern" world — to tailor the demands of religion to fit the contingencies of the age. But this temptation also has been felt within the household of the faith. It was yielded to in the nineteenth century by the Abbé Lamennais, and it was the basis of the Modernist movement at the beginning of the twentieth century. This is the historic temptation of the liberal.

Both temptations are a betrayal of the Church and of the world — that world which the Church strives to save. As Christians, we betray our vocation if we succumb to either.

The extreme conservative merely rejects — his answer to the world is a simple no; the extreme liberal merely accepts — his answer to the world is a simple yes. If I may make a theological analogy, I would say that the extreme conservative, who merely rejects the world, analogically commits the sin of despair; and the extreme liberal, who says a simple yes to the world, analogically commits the sin of presumption. Christian wisdom rejects both. Christian wisdom demands that in our response to the world we find a middle way. The ancient adage of Christian wisdom, "Virtus stat in media," "Strength stands in the middle," is as true here as it is in other aspects of our vocation as Christian citizens of an earthly city.

Although this question of the relationship of the believer to the age is a perennial problem, older than the Christian church, it is a particularly acute problem in our own age; and it promises to become even more acute in any age that we can foresee, because we live not only in a post-Christian age, but also in what is probably a post-religious age.

It is very easy, and very comforting, to talk about a "religious revival" in America — about the strength of the Church and the strength of the parishes in our land. We can take comfort in religious statistics, however, only if we fail to understand what is really happening in the world about us. Almost everywhere in the world, religion is in retreat. It is on the defensive. The world that is now being made is a world from which, tragically, religion is largely absent. And so, for the believer the question, "How shall I sing the Lord's song in a strange land?" is more pressing today than it was two hundred years ago; and it will be even more pressing in the future.

The question that Mr. Buckley and I are debating, therefore, is not an academic one; it is very real. And it is not a new one; it is very ancient. It is a question that we can ignore only at great peril for religion itself. Because, since the French Revolution of 1789 (that watershed of history) the Christian, more than at any other time, perhaps, since the fall of the Roman empire, has been forced, if he is to survive, to make a radical reassessment of his position toward the age and of his relationship to the power structures of the world.

This is the problem of conservative and liberal Catholicism. In making this reassessment, what should the Catholic's attitude be? What should his adjustment be, if any? Should he reject out of hand? Should he embrace? Should he attempt to find a middle way?

Now, I maintain that this problem is particularly acute, and the temptations particularly strong, for those Catholics in the modern world who call themselves "conservative." They have tended toward a complete rejection of the world that comes out of the French Revolution. They have tended to view the modern age simply as the dominion of the Prince of Darkness, and to say: "We have our oasis of truth. Here we will stay, and our only contact with the outside world will be to issue an occasional communiqué condemning it."

Such an attitude among Catholics presents terrible problems for the Church, if only from the standpoint of the Church's evangelizing mission. And it presents terrible problems for the Christian layman whose personal vocation, even as a layman, is to save the world. In the epistle for the mass of the twentieth Sunday after Pentecost, St. Paul tells us, "See, brethren, that you walk carefully; not as fools but as wise men, redeeming the time, because the days are evil." We note that St. Paul did not tell us to castigate the time. He told us to "redeem the time." And here, in the fifth chapter of Ephesians, St. Paul briefly summed up what is the Christian's vocation in every age — to find himself in evil times and yet not to turn his back upon them but redeem them.

This certainly is relevant to one of the really horrifying things about our modern condition — the polarity that exists in modern culture between the world and religion — between Man and God. In the words of a great contemporary Protestant theologian, Paul Tillich: "The modern world sees Christianity as reaction pure and simple; and Christians see the modern world as rebellion pure and simple." In this tragic situation neither can effectively address a word to the other. And so, what has actually been happening under our very eyes and what is continuing to happen, at an even faster pace, is that the world goes on building its city, from which we, as Christians, are absent; and we Christians, smug in our own wisdom and in our own virtue, are content to let that city, quite literally, go to hell.

Father John Courtney Murray, one of the most distinguished contemporary Catholic theologians, addressed himself to this problem a few years ago when he asked whether, in the face of modern secular civilization, the Catholic's attitude should be to stand fast, holding out his hand in an attempt to stop this civilization's progress, all the while looking over his shoulder at the ever diminishing figure of Isabella II of Spain. "What a peculiar stance for the universal Church," Father Murray observed.

My criticism of those Catholics who call themselves conservatives is that they do precisely this. In their major attitudes toward modern civilization, in the last one hundred and fifty years, they have been vehemently negative. And in this, I think, they have helped to create that image of the Church as a mere nay-sayer which pervades the modern world. This image is essentially a caricature of the Church, but it prevents modern men, almost en masse, from seeing the Church as that community of creative love and salvation which the Church really is. Historically, too many Catholic conservatives have fallen into a habit of mere nostalgia, of mere defensiveness; they have thus seemed, at least, unconcerned for any of the great battles for which the modern world has fought. With Father Murray I would say: what a peculiar stance for the universal Church!

It seems to me that the error of conservative Catholicism has been its failure to distinguish — and whatever may be the intellectual failures of Catholics, the last should be a failure to distinguish! And, because of their failure to distinguish, conservative Catholics have condemned everything for which the modern world has struggled because the *reasons* for which the modern world has struggled have been wrong. Who in the modern world, for example, has fought the great battles for equality and freedom? (These are easy words, I know.) Concretely, who has fought the battles for racial justice? Was it the Catholics of Europe who stood most strongly against anti-Semitism? In this country, has it been Catholics who have led the battle for Negro rights? No, in both cases it has been the despised liberals. Who has fought the battles for freedom of the press and for freedom of conscience? Has the Catholic community either in this country or in Europe been famous for these things? I fear the answer is obvious. And again it is no.

The picture of modern history is largely the opposite. The Catholic community, on the whole, has either held back from the battles through indifference or has been content to condemn those who fought for these causes because their philosophy was a secularist, a non-Christian or even anti-Christian philosophy. But if the modern world has fought these battles for the wrong reasons, it seems to me that in these matters the Christian's proper role should be to supply the right reasons, rather than to turn his back upon the battles themselves.

Certainly, in modern history the battleground for the major arguments between liberal and conservative Catholics has been France. It was French conservative Catholics who, through the entire nineteenth century, insisted on involving the fortunes of the Church with the fortunes of the French monarchy. And it was a great "liberal" pope, Leo XIII, who finally ordered these conservative Catholics to cease tying the hopes of the Church to anachronistic political institutions and admonished them to come to terms with the republican institutions of their age, if they were to have any hope of speaking to their age at all.

Again, in our century, it was another pope, Pius XI, who condemned the conservative French political movement, L'Action Française. In this movement conservative Catholics once more sought to tie the Church to a rightest nationalism. At the cost of great bitterness among many Catholics, Pius XI demanded that they cease their efforts to involve the Church with authoritarian politics.

And we may recall the recent, poignant letter that close to two hundred Spanish priests circulated among their bishops, warning of a dark future for the Church in Spain unless, more than they had in the past, Spanish Catholics entered into and showed some concern for the causes of social injustice and civil liberties — causes for which, once again, the Spanish liberals seem to be struggling alone.

In considering these things, in our tendency to damn causes for which we should have fought (and which should now be our causes) because they are the causes of men with whose philosophy we cannot agree, we might recall the wisdom of John Henry Newman, who once observed: "If they say to me, this cannot be Christian because it is found in paganism, I reply, this cannot be pagan because it is found in Christianity."

In these matters the Catholic liberal distinguishes. He recalls the words of the contemporary French theologian, Henri de Lubac, who has reminded us that in every age the Christian has a dual vocation. He faces two tasks: to conserve and to adapt. If he merely conserves and fails to adapt, then he has betrayed his duty as a Christian to the world. I believe it is the tragedy of conservative Catholicism that it has so completely polarized itself, and built such thick walls around itself, that it has forsaken the Christian's second vocation, which is to adapt the truths he has conserved to the unique needs of the present.

The Catholic liberal, however, believes that God's providence did not stop at some point in history — in the sixteenth century at the Reformation or in 1789 at the Revolution. He believes that God works *through* history. Because our God is a God of history, and He does bring good even out of evil.

It was a nineteenth-century French theologian, Dupanloup, the bishop of Orleans, who said something that I think we should remember today. He asked what Catholics should say to the men of our age — the liberals, the secularists — who accuse us of reaction and of failure to accept the facts of modern liberty. Dupanloup replied: "We must say this: we accept, we welcome the liberties for which you have fought. You made the Revolution without us. Indeed you made it against us; but you also made it for us. In spite of you, God willed it so."

Modern liberalism has fought and won battles for which we Catholics should have fought but which, in our blindness, we too often opposed. Thus does God's providence work in man's affairs. Those Catholics who are described as "liberal" — who are "open" toward modern civilization — are at their best, I think, when they are in search for the evidences of God's providence in history, even in movements where they may least expect to find God's hand.

The Troubling Spirit

━ "But still we have a wisdom to offer those who have reached maturity: not a philosophy of our age, it is true, still less of the masters of our age. . . . We teach what scripture calls 'the things that no eye has seen and no ear has heard, things beyond the mind of man, all that God has prepared for those who love him' (1 Cor. 2)."

The crisis and, one must say, the agony into which the Church has entered since Pope Paul VI issued *Humanae vitae* are not, of course, about birth control. The birth control question is merely the catalyst that has forced us to face polarities and problems that have been growing in the Church since the beginnings of Vatican II. The real crisis is one of authority and freedom, and the agony it brings with it is shared by those who think they must now defend one of these values against the other, and those many more who are tragically torn between the two.

If the time of troubles now upon us is to be a time for growth, through the Spirit, in the Church, this real crisis and the shared quality of its agony must be quickly grasped. For though the birth control "debate" within the Church as we know it has indeed ended, our crisis has just begun. It will finally work to the good of the Church only if we recognize that the agony it brings with it *is* shared by men who oppose each other out of an equal love for the Church.

Commonweal, 23 August 1968

What we see in the Church today are the beginnings of a drama that has been played out in civil societies for the past 160 years — since the French Revolution, at least. The claims of authority versus the rights of individual conscience; the necessity for continuity versus the need for change; the demands of order versus the expression of freedom: these have been the great conflicts, the great polarities, of modern societies, and they have finally invaded the Church. That we kept them out for so long was a miracle of our ancient stability that could not endure forever. Our peace has seemed increasingly unreal, and our crisis was bound to come.

But if we in the Church can learn from other crises of authority and freedom that have been lived out in modern secular societies, we must know that the way to tragedy and disaster lies precisely in the failure of opposing parties to recognize their shared and bedrock concerns, their shared loyalty and love, even in the midst of their disagreements. In civil society values seemingly opposed must be held together in tension, and so too in the Church. Tyranny or chaos — the dissolution of society itself — are invited when the defenders of a particular value see the defenders of an "opposed" value as The Enemy and seek the future of society only through the total triumph of their own cause.

What has been emerging in the Church in this decade, and is now fully in view, is a situation that reminds us of these things. If in the crisis now upon us the defenders of "authority" see dissent from the conclusions of *Humanae vitae* as disloyalty and subversion, and spokesmen for a new Christian "freedom" view defenders of the magisterium as simply obscurantist or "irrelevant," then all possibility of creative tension is ended and the stage for schism is set. "Betrayal of the Church" in the present crisis will be precisely by those, on either side, who seek further to polarize opinion and thus close themselves to the possibility of the Spirit's working through a time of trouble to bring forth a new synthesis of values.

The crisis that now seizes us has, of course, been smoldering for over a century, waiting its historical moment to erupt. Only those lacking a sense of history could think it was "caused" by the birth control controversy or would disappear were all Catholics docilely to accept the conclusions of *Humanae vitae*. A hundred years ago, in the great Ultramontane-Liberal Catholic struggles of the mid-nineteenth century, the outline of our unresolved conflict was composed. William George Ward wrote in 1869 that the test of Catholic loyalty was "to live as it were in an atmosphere of authority; to look for direction at every moment towards the Church and towards the Vicar of Christ." But John Henry Newman, who was horrified by such views, after he had been made a cardinal offered his famous reply to a toast to the pope: "I drink to the Pope — but I drink to Conscience first."

Newman knew that the dichotomy between authority and freedom posed by Ultramontanes was a false one, and that the hope of Catholicism for the future lay in the creation of new relationships between them. Such a creation he knew would be painful — and made even more painful than it need be by "party men." But he looked to theologians who would refuse to join any party and who, aware of historical and theological complexities, seek new understandings of the proper roles and limits of both authority and freedom — gifts that must always coexist in tension within the Church. And such is now clearly the task of all who wish to serve the needs not of a party nor of an immediate moment but who seek the evolution of a new *Catholic* synthesis of values.

In 1867 the aging Newman wrote to Ward from the Birmingham Oratory: "You are making a Church within a Church, as the Novatians of old did within the Catholic pale, and as, outside the Catholic pale, the Evangelicals of the Establishment. As they talk of 'vital religion' and vital 'doctrines' and will not allow that their brethren 'know the Gospel' or are Gospel preachers, unless they profess the small shibboleths of their own sect, so you are doing your best to make a party in the Catholic Church, and in St. Paul's words are dividing Christ by exalting your opinions into Dogmas."

Sectarianism is a narrow and limited response to immediate and short-term problems. Lacking any sense of history or of complexity, it may achieve certain quick victories and answer certain felt needs, but it soon is lost and forgotten in the boundless oceans of time. It thus stands as the eternal enemy of any genuine Catholicism which, of its very nature, is universal, long-range, and complex. And the sectarianism of "party men" is what threatens the Church — the *Catholic* Church — today. Those who see the present crisis in simple terms of *either* authority or freedom — not realizing that the very nature of the crisis demands new understandings and limits for both authority and freedom within the Church — are sectarians. From them and from their fervors may God deliver us.

It is somewhat worse than pointless, for example, for defenders of the magisterium to demand acceptance of all the conclusions of *Humanae vitae* in the name of authority when authority, its exercise and its limits, is precisely the question, along with the question of the exercise and limits of freedom, that must now be reconsidered in the Church. And it is somewhat worse than irresponsible for defenders of freedom to argue as though freedom were a value that exists within the Church in splendid isolation, unrelated to the nature and functions of the magisterium.

A time of crisis should be a time of learning — and this, perhaps, is an historic moment when the learning Church and the teaching Church can meet in a radically new encounter. There must be authority in the Church; but how simple is it and how complex? How single and how multiple? How centered and how diverse? From whom and from what does the teaching Church learn, and what does it learn? Who and what must it consult — what kind of consensus must it discover — before it can function as the teaching Church, and then what are the limits to what it can teach with an authority binding on all the People of God? Those things delivered unto it "that no eye has seen and no ear heard, things beyond the mind of man, all that God has prepared for those who love him": surely and infallibly it can and must teach these things. But the philosophy of this or any other age? Or politics or economics? Or individual moral choice, beyond the statement of general principles?

These are questions we must finally and honestly face, all the time holding multiple values in focus, confident that the Spirit works in the Church even in a time of acrimony, confusion, and pain — indeed, that our present trouble may be the Spirit's movement bringing to birth new things in the Church. For the Spirit is a troubling Spirit and he shakes us from easy securities to see that the path of the Church through history is a pilgrim's way.

The whole direction of modern thought and culture, for example, has been toward limiting areas of authority and extending areas of freedom. It is the process Bonhoeffer identified as "the coming of age of humanity." Vast parts of human life once regarded as provinces for the exercise of paternal direction by the Church or by the state are now accepted as the proper domain of an individual's conscience. Thus has man's hard won dignity as a *choosing* being been achieved. The Church, no more than any civil society, can escape from this direction, nor can the Church fail forever to reconsider her traditional understanding of the limits of her authority in light of this earned experience of the race.

And yet, having said this, we must say at the same time that authority within the Church is a gift, divinely granted and not able to be humanly revoked. To bring these truths together in new understandings, and in charity, is the task to which we are called today in the Church. We have avoided this task for too long. But the questions of authority and freedom in the Church can never be thought of again as they were before July 1968. This, in God's plan, may be the indispensable service rendered to the Church by *Humanae vitae.*

Commitment on Campus:
Pittsburgh/Carnegie-Mellon

▬ Pittsburgh is a special kind of city. It has a history that predates the revolutionary war and a tradition that combines elements of the East (of which it is an outpost) and of the West (to which it is the gate). It is a city set down in the midst of (and, in parts, on top of) great topographical splendors; and it has an architecture that is both indigenous and unique.

An entrenched, closed, and very White–Anglo-Saxon–Protestant aristocracy presides over the city's cultural and economic life; but this life is worked out practically through a dazzling variety of self-conscious, self-contained, and largely non-Protestant ethnic groups. Pittsburgh is not a sophisticated city (no serious bookstore, theater, or even restaurant can be found in the town); but it is an interesting city in the pluralism and vibrancy of its forms.

In the midst of its Civic Center — Oakland — two institutions of higher learning — the University of Pittsburgh and Carnegie-Mellon University — flourish. They flourish, that is, in wide areas of liberal, scientific, professional, and technical knowledge. Something about almost anything can be studied in these universities. Something about almost anything, that is, except religion or theology. God is not officially dead in these schools;

he is, in fact, conjured up (in the form of his luckless ministers) to grace such occasional happenings as commencements and memorial services. Yet, for the most part, the Deity, and the fact that men have thought and said profound or foolish things about him through the ages, are subjects politely ignored.

Neither of Pittsburgh's major universities maintains a department of theology or comparative religion; nor, from a reading of their catalogues, would one guess that religion has had a significant influence on man's social, esthetic, psychological, political, and intellectual life. This says something about the provincialism and quaint rationalism of Pittsburgh itself. The provincialism is more evident at the University of Pittsburgh and the rationalism is more obvious at Carnegie-Mellon, but both institutions share symptoms of each malaise.

The University of Pittsburgh is a paradigm of curious anomalies. From its beginning the school was private and nonsectarian; and it has been deeply influenced by the Pittsburgh Protestant aristocracy who were its major backers. In 1967, however, the university became "state-related"; and while other state-related universities in Pennsylvania — most notably Temple and Penn State — have, in the past few years, developed full, distinguished, and ecumenical departments of theology and comparative religion, the University of Pittsburgh has not.

The only course open to undergraduates that deals seriously with contemporary theological issues appears, as it were, in disguise: this is the course in Existentialism taught by the Jewish theologian Richard Rubinstein. It is offered in the *French* department — and it is one of the most consistently over-enrolled electives in the entire undergraduate curriculum.

If the condition of theological education at the University of Pittsburgh seems culturally arrested, however, the hopes for such education at Carnegie-Mellon University are yet to be born. Carnegie-Mellon has recently emerged from the status of an in-

stitute of technology to the dignity of a university; and one religion course – dealing rather predictably, with the "crisis" of
religion today – is offered in its history department.

This limited or indifferent attitude of both these universities
toward religion has, of course, a profound effect on their students. Most of them are not "religious" in a sense that older
generations would easily understand and accept. Yet like students everywhere today, they are concerned and many of them,
deeply troubled. They are a questioning generation, disinher-
ited of its own tradition (which it has no chance to know) and
in search of surrogates for it. "Religion," to many of them, means
simply fear, with "God" as a cosmic J. Edgar Hoover and "the
Church" as his F.B.I.

In desperation for meaning, they turn to various forms of oc-
cultism or the esoteric (astrology, even, and Eastern religions
are very popular with many who are almost completely ignorant
of the Judeo-Christian tradition); or they read Kahlil Gibran's
The Prophet or, more seriously, Eric Fromm's *The Art of Loving* and find some meaning and hope in these things. Others
turn simply to cynicism, negation, and protest.

Many students, finding that their universities offer them little
or nothing to learn about what a man or God might be, come
to the several religious chaplaincies in an almost pleading search
for value and meaning – and for an education that cannot be
found in their schools. Most of these students have read Al-
bert Camus. (He remains the modern "religious" author for the
generation.) Many of them have read, or at least read about,
Teilhard de Chardin, and all of them know about Harvey Cox's
The Secular City.

The rare and deeply concerned minority are willing – at great
personal cost to their time and energy – to take nonaccredited
courses and meet for serious theological reading and discussion
groups, at the Oratory, the center of the University Parish of

the Pittsburgh Catholic Diocese, which Bishop John Wright established eight years ago. A group of graduate students from the University of Pittsburgh came to me recently to ask for a serious course in the thought of John Henry Newman.

Last year large numbers of them came to the Oratory on Wednesday nights for a seminar in modern theology. They read Newman, Berdyaev, Barth, Teilhard, and Henri de Lubac. On alternate Friday nights of each month through the year amazing numbers of graduate students (an average of fifty to ninety) crowd into the Oratory for an entire evening of mass and group discussions.

Other groups of students and faculty come to the Oratory every night of the week (except Sunday) in efforts to understand for the first time, or to recover, their own religious and theological tradition. A group of younger faculty members organized itself this year to make a serious study of St. Augustine, and literally hundreds of undergraduates, graduates, and faculty members have come to the Oratory during the past months to borrow or even buy copies of the new "Dutch Catechism."

Increasingly, these seminars and group discussions tend to be "ecumenical." At the Friday night graduate-student Mass and discussions, for example, there are now always a sizable minority of Protestant students and also students who would profess no religion at all. Few of them — Catholic or Protestant — feel sure of their positions in a way that earlier generations felt sure, but they are hungry for meaning and anxious with questions. The gratitude of many of them is deep when they discover that the theological tradition of Western man is viable and relevant for them, if only they are given some opportunity as adults to learn it.

The University of Pittsburgh and Carnegie-Mellon University are not unique in their failure to provide this opportunity. The roots of the failure lie deep in the American secularist-rationalist tradition itself. But other universities, in Pennsylvania and across the nation, are now attempting to fill the theological void and offer their students an opportunity, at least, for critical study of man's ultimate concerns.

One waits and wonders when the word will reach Pittsburgh's universities that something basic is lacking in their educational structures and that the void can be filled only by a conversion from provincialism and rationalism within themselves.

God in Every Pot

━━ Patriotism, Samuel Johnson said, is the last refuge of a scoun-
drel. Religion, in the rhetoric of American politics, is surely the
first refuge of self-righteous patriotism.

One of the persistent and depressing obscenities in our national life is the use made by politicians of what Winston Churchill called "the God bit."

American statesmen invoke the Deity to cast a smokescreen
of rectitude over their fumblings toward survival. The prestige
of the Almighty's high office is used to canonize policies that,
at best, are reasonably enlightened but, at worst, are cynically
immoral.

In the name of a principle — separation of church and state —
we deny the use of public funds for the teaching of purely secular subjects in church-related schools. But we seem to expect
our presidents to worship publicly each Sunday, and our presidents, in turn, find it easy and unembarrassing to suggest God's
support for their policies — from the waging of wars against "God-
less" enemies to the granting of pardon to a predecessor whose
crimes have been neither cited nor acknowledged.

Dwight D. Eisenhower instituted the practice of opening his
cabinet meetings with prayer and, during his administration,
much of the official rhetoric of the cold war invoked poor God
as an American ally.

The New York Times, 1 October 1974

During John F. Kennedy's brief tenure, God was discreetly kept off White House invitations lists, but during Richard M. Nixon's administration the White House was turned, once a week, into an interdenominational chapel.

There, on most Sundays, scrubbed worshipers heard respectable clergymen preach comfortable sermons on those moral virtues Mr. Nixon tried so hard to put forward as the mark of his administration. Mr. Nixon himself, at the conclusion of his first major address on the Watergate affair, piously called down God's blessing upon his listeners.

And now Gerald R. Ford shows signs of surpassing his predecessors in reliance on the Deity's advice. His pronouncements to date imply that God is a member of his policy-planning staff.

His first address to the Congress suggested that, following the Nixon trauma, no atheists were left in America, and in the text of his statement of pardon for Mr. Nixon, God and prayer are woven in as threads of grace, holding together, and giving ultimate sanction to, a decision otherwise compounded of human elements.

The bishop of Rome—the pope—styles himself "servant of the servants of God." By suggesting, in his pardon statement, that his decision was inspired by convictions he felt "not as President, but as a humble servant of God," Mr. Ford again theologizes politics and introduces into presidential preachment an analogue to the papal style itself.

Both the religious and the nonreligious should demand an end to such nonsense. Neither God nor man is honored or well served by it.

It is a truism to observe that we live in a postreligious world and that continuing political effort to elicit the support of a hidden God (whose ways are mysterious) is worse than an anachronism; it is blasphemous misuse of what religious men regard as sacred.

Now, that which is sacred cannot be casually approached or touched. Certainly it cannot be "used" or marketed. The sacred can be spoken of only with reticence and awe. It cannot be made the easy associate of men's designs.

In the public policy and style of a secular society, God should not be invoked as a convenience or cited as a platitude. God, by any theological definition, is *not* comfortable.

The dangers of continuing the present stance of public piety in Washington are real. First, "God" is made an accessory to the sordid as well as the noble facts of our national life. Second, the implications are clear that only believing, churchgoing citizens are "true" Americans.

The first is a debasement of God and his freedom; the second is a diminution of man and his freedom. The one is antireligious; the other is antihuman.

Presidents grant pardon for the crimes and follies of their fellow citizens, even unrepentant predecessors in office. But if God is made a partner in such matters, who shall grant a pardon to God?

REVIEWS AND REFLECTIONS

Leisure in a Bourgeois World

▰ The popular notion of leisure as an opportunity for "escape" leaves many deeply puzzled by the words of the psalmist: "Have leisure and know that I'm God." In order to understand the words we must recover a loftier, more classical concept of leisure as an affirmative condition (the very opposite of idleness) by which man transcends the world of work and, having transcended it, is enabled to contemplate those things which lie beyond it — himself, the universe, and God.

This concept of leisure is one of the foundations of Western culture, more, one of the indispensable conditions without which man is something less than man — a mere worker, a functionary, a thing. It is the subject of a brilliant examination in two essays by the German philosopher Joseph Pieper, now published under the title *Leisure the Basis of Culture.*

The first and title essay is a profound investigation, historically and sociologically, into the nature of leisure itself. The second essay, "The Philosophical Act," studies philosophy as leisure's highest good, the human act par exellence. This essay is a logical extension of the first because, as Dr. Pieper observes, philosophy, which is the eternal search for wisdom, presupposes "silence, a contemplative attention to things, in which man begins to see how worthy of reverence they really are."

The basis for both essays is the author's thesis: "Culture depends for its very foundation on leisure, and leisure, in its turn, is not possible unless it has a durable and living link with the *cultus,* with divine worship." A quotation from Plato, which introduces the essays, remarkably illustrates the antique origins and classical importance of this thesis: "But the gods, taking pity on mankind, born to work, laid down the succession of recurring feasts to restore them from their fatigues . . . so that nourishing themselves in festive companionship with the gods, they should again stand upright and erect." The nature of leisure is thus basically united to contemplation in the great tradition of Western culture, and both are dependent on a real awareness of the transcendent and the Divine. Here lies the secret of freedom.

The difficulty is that modern civilization has placed the idea of leisure in double jeopardy: the triumph of a purely utilitarian social idealism has left little room and less regard for a concept which produces nothing immediate and concrete toward "progress"; the very idea of a "leisure class" has fallen into disrepute as an aristocratic anachronism, something incompatible with egalitarianism. And the growing externalization of life, the almost universal phenomenon of an activist mass culture, has emptied the virtue of contemplation of any meaning for the majority of modern men, and left them dismally unprepared to cope with leisure in the few moments when they may still have an opportunity for it.

Boredom and ennui, a frantic search for diversion, are the common reactions to an hour, or a day, of quiet. The modern Cleopatra in Eliot's *Waste Land* desperately asking "What shall I do now? What shall I do? . . . What shall we do tomorrow? What shall we ever do?" undoubtedly gives voice to one of contemporary man's most pathetic problems. Manufacturers of television sets and producers of endless third-rate movies have made their fortunes providing an answer, an answer itself symptomatic of the problem.

It does not seem far-fetched to speculate that future historians may mark down this disappearance of any popular regard for or understanding of the nature of leisure, and, at the same time, the near hysterical search for external diversion, as one of the major cultural crises of modern civilization. And there can be little doubt that it followed upon the victory of the bourgeois spirit (with all that this implies) over the older Hellenistic-Judeo-Christian tradition of Western culture. For leisure, and its highest goal, contemplation, lie at the heart of this tradition, but they are eternal strangers to bourgeois value.

In his memorable essay, "The Bourgeois Mind," Nicholas Berdyaev has defined the state of being bourgeois as a state distinguished by its particular "soullessness," its constitutional inability to comprehend the heroic and the transcendent. Consequently, the genuine bourgeois, to the extent that he is a bourgeois, is at heart the enemy of Christ. Berdyaev quotes Léon Bloy's bitter aside on bourgeois religiosity: "The Lord Jesus is very decorative in shop windows."

When the bourgeois is a social reformer, when he occupies himself with building a "better world," he reduces man to a functionary, a thing, and robs him of that unique dignity and freedom which consist in his transcending the realm of "things." The totality of reality is thus something to be used rather than something to be *reverenced*, and concepts such as leisure and contemplation lose all meaning, become, indeed, a scandal. Both God and man are exiles from a bourgeois world.

So complete has been the triumph of the bourgeois spirit in the modern world that, in Christopher Dawson's words, "we are all more or less bourgeois, and our civilization is bourgeois from top to bottom." To look for the bourgeois, then, in one economic group or in some particular ideological faction is to mistake the nature of the bourgeois spirit, which is a universal one. (It is ironic that the "bourgeois" is the favorite whipping boy of Marxist propaganda, but, once the true nature of the bourgeois spirit is understood, Marxism must appear as its terrible, but final and logical *reductio ad absurdum*.) The bourgeois spirit is everywhere, in the schools, in the press, in the legislatures, in the churches. It is found among rich and poor, among capitalists and Communists, among Catholics and Protestants and Jews.

This triumph of the bourgeois spirit has witnessed the almost universal acceptance of the bourgeois virtues — the virtues of the practical and immediately useful, of work for work's own sake, of the "rational." We need only consult our own experience to realize the extent of this triumph in our world and the extreme difficulty of rejecting its implications.

We live in a world which has come under the control of a "mystique of work," and we are all, more or less, wedded to the practical. A "good" education is one which prepares one for a "good" job, and a "good" job is one which pays lots of money. A successful man is one who has accumulated a significant amount of the world's goods and "used" them in a practical way.

Joseph Pieper defines the proletarian as "the man who is fettered to the process of work." Every man whose life is completely filled by his work, he tells us, "is a proletarian because his life has shrunk inwardly, and contracted, with the result that he can no longer act significantly outside his work, and perhaps can no longer even conceive of such a thing."

Thus defined, the great majority of modern men are proletarians; the mystique of work controls more and more of life. Leisure itself, in this world, becomes a mere necessary stop between rounds of work and its value is seen as preparing us to work more efficiently on the morrow. It is at once an escape from work and a prelude to more work. Civilization thus progresses toward the level of the beehive.

"It is necessary for the perfection of human society," Aquinas wrote, "that there should be men who devote their lives to contemplation." Bourgeois civilization, in failing to understand and value the true meaning and lofty dignity of leisure, has lost the concept of contemplation, and, in so doing, has lost the concept of man. For it is in leisure, genuinely understood, that man rises above the level of a thing to be used and enters the realm where he can be at home with the potentialities of his own nature, where, with no concern for *doing*, no ties to the immediate, the particular, and the practical, he can attend to the love of wisdom, can begin leading a truly human life. Thus, transcending the world of work, man ceases to be a proletarian. He begins to function as man.

"There is one institution in the world," Pieper reminds us, "which forbids useful activity and servile work on particular days, and in this way prepares, as it were, a sphere for non-proletarian existence." The Church, through her liturgy and cycles of feasts, invites man to that leisure and contemplation where he can again "stand upright and erect." It provides one of the last remaining refuges from a workaday bourgeois world.

Leisure the Basis of Culture is a profound and rich book. It should remind us that if we become so engaged in the activities connected with "saving" Western civilization that, in the process, we lose what capacity for leisure is left us, then we can never "save" Western civilization at all, but only that dreary counterfeit, the world of the bourgeois functionary. We will have prepared the way for the final and universal reign of the subhuman.

The Man Outside:
The Prose Works of Wolfgang Borchert

■ Gabriel Marcel reminds us that in whatever direction we may look today it is hard to escape the fact that we have entered upon what Christians might describe as an eschatological age. Terrible force is given to his reminder in a place where man's capacity for final self-destruction was as evident as in postwar Germany. Here it was impossible to escape the spectre of annihilation; no matter to what perfumed sanctuary one might retreat, the stench of death would follow.

The imaginative man forced to function in such a milieu is exposed to a unique temptation, not to seek a deliverance from death but rather a surrender to it which carries some shred of meaning. Wolfgang Borchert was a young German who sought such a meaning. Born in 1921, soldier and sufferer on the Russian front during the bitter campaigns of 1941, confined in a Nazi prison during the later years of the war, he returned to his native Hamburg in 1945. There he found a city whose ruin was a nightmare symbol of what had happened to his whole generation, more tragically "lost" than any other in history. He died in Hamburg in 1947. In his prose works, now published in this country, he left his anguished commentary on the world of "nothing."

Commonweal, 25 April 1952

"Who will write us new laws of harmony?" Borchert asked. "We have no further use for well-tempered clavichords. We ourselves are too much dissonance." This search for the principled annihilation lies at the center of his work. The title piece, *The Man Outside,* was described by the author as "a play which no theater will produce and no public will want to see." (It became one of the most widely produced and discussed plays in Germany after Borchert's death, and was three times presented over the BBC.)

The drama is set in the author's home, Hamburg, and tells of a returned soldier to whom all doors are closed, whom even death rejects when, in despair, he seeks a too easy solution through suicide in the Elbe. (Death's taunt "I spit on your suicide" surely represents an ultimate in humiliation and defeat.) Even God here suffers the fate of all else. Reduced to a pathetic impotence, He appears as a helpless old man, weeping over but powerless to assist His "poor children." The only voice heard in the defense of life is the voice of "the Other," a symbol of all that has been and will be left behind. But "the Other" can offer no reason for living beyond "life itself," a highly unconvincing reason in the context of postwar Hamburg, and so we are left with a final nihilism.

Most of the stories are very short and compact. The half-mad soldier, nicknamed, "Jesus," whose duty it is to try graves for size, the young prisoner whose only remaining contact with life is a dandelion which he finds in the yard, the soldier on the eastern front who fondles a piece of pink cloth cut from his sweetheart's petticoat (all that is left of a world which still contained love), these are the figures of Borchert's apocalypse.

Borchert's work indicates that he was primarily a poet; one looks in vain for the novelist's technical accomplishments; the sense for movement and the ability to objectify experience are absent from these stories. They are, more properly, extended metaphors, each communicating, through symbol, something of the dreadful immediacy of the catastrophe in which the poet played his part. There is no concern with abstract problems in these stories, no questioning of "war guilt" or interests in the reasons for the catastrophe. Man is beyond rationalizing, just as he is beyond tragedy. For with the death of civilization and the advent of "nothing" has come the death of reason, of feeling, and of tragedy. When the final curtain falls, "worms and fish break into noiseless applause."

George Santayana

━ In the celebrated "definition" with which he concluded his discourse on "Knowledge and Religious Duty," John Henry Newman observed that the "gentleman," even if he be an unbeliever, will yet be "too profound and large minded to ridicule religion or to act against it." He will, rather, be a man "who respects piety and devotion" and supports institutions as "venerable, beautiful or useful to which he cannot give his assent."

And though his ideal natural "gentleman" may not be an orthodox Christian, the cardinal continued, he will probably embrace a personal type of religion: "In that case his religion is one of imagination and sentiment; it is the embodiment of those ideas of the sublime, majestic and beautiful, without which there can be no large philosophy."

This ideal of the magnanimous man unillumined by revelation might well serve as the epitaph of George Santayana, the maganimous man *par excellence* of our century, whose death in Rome on September 27 has left us all much poorer. For with a brilliance and a dedication which has become a contemporary legend, Santayana lived and symbolized that "life of reason" which is Western humanism's highest natural goal.

Twenty years ago, at his last public appearance, Santayana asked an audience of philosophers gathered at The Hague to commemorate the tercentenary of Spinoza's birth, "provision-

Commonweal, 10 October 1952

ally, for an hour, and without prejudice to your ulterior reasonable convictions, to imagine the truth to be as unfavorable as possible to your desires, and as contrary as possible to your presumptions; so that the spirit in each of us may be drawn away from its accidental home and subjected to an utter denudation and supreme trial."

This request was no accident of rhetorical flourish: Santayana's whole intellectual and spiritual life was such a denudation and trial. His skepticism was so compelling that it shaped all his speculations to the conclusion that the truth could not be as he wished it to be. He could never postulate as *real* those things for which, as *ideals*, he had sworn eternal friendship.

This constitutional pessimism, stoically accepted and philosophically refined, prevented his ever, in this life, finding for his ideals a local habitation and concrete name. And so, though he loved and honored the Christian revelation and the Catholic Church above all things, he could not bring himself, finally, to accept them philosophically; they seemed to him simply too good to be true. The result was that remarkable detachment, nostalgia, and regret which distinguished all his work.

"For my own part," Santayana wrote of his youth, "I was quite certain that life was not worth living; for if religion was false everything was worthless; and almost everything if religion were true. . . . I saw the same alternative between Catholicism and complete disillusion; but I was never afraid of disillusion, and I have chosen it."

But Santayana's early disillusion did not turn, as in the case of some others, to bitterness or mockery. His genius was consecrated to the service of the Good, the Beautiful, and the True, as, given the exigencies of his temperament, he could conceive them. His role as the spiritually homeless man was part of his deep participation in the tragic sense of life. His sorrow in this role is commemorated in one of his autobiographical sonnets, in which he assures us that although he stands outside the Church he would enter could he honestly do so:

> some are born to stand perplexed aside
> From so much sorrow . . . of whom I am one.

This standing "perplexed aside" was a unique and often misunderstood mission in a world torn by factions and fanaticisms. But Santayana's loyalties were pledged to ideals of the imagination and intellect which knew neither time nor place. His refusal to commit himself to the present made him an anomaly in this most committed of centuries, and his inability to place his religious idealism where it logically belonged left him a philosopher strangely incomplete. But, in the designs of Divine Providence, he may have played a singularly valuable role in the drama of our time.

Santayana would have felt at home in Plato's Academy, and if we are to hope for our civilization at all we must believe that the triumph of activism and utilitarianism will never be so complete that the classically detached and intellectually disinterested man will have no lesson to teach the future.

George Santayana's life reminds us of things which, if we forget, we are lost. His example was incomplete, but within its sphere it was unparalleled in its magnificence. We must now hope that there awaits him, for all eternity, the contemplation face-to-face of that Reality which, as an ideal, he loved so long. May perpetual light shine upon him.

Sean O'Faolain's Newman's Way:
The Odyssey of John Henry Newman

━━ John Henry Newman once affirmed that for him there existed two (and only two) obviously self-luminous beings: himself and God; and for his epitaph he chose a motto which underlined his constitutional disbelief in the reality of material things in the face of eternal spiritual value: *ex umbris et imaginibus in veritatem.*

Mr. O'Faolain's study of Newman's "way," from his earliest childhood up to his submission to the Roman Catholic Church, is a brilliant inquiry into the basis of his subject's genius and lifelong isolation. "There can have been few more lonely men in the world than the aging Newman," O'Faolain writes in his epilogue. Indeed, there can have been, because there can have been few more lonely in their youth.

This present work, with a rare combination of original scholarship, imagination, sensitivity, and humor, indicates why, in a certain sense, Newman's "odyssey" never ended, until, after ninety years of life, he finally passed from those "shadows and images" which were his constant present into that Truth which only eternity could fully reveal.

Newman's "way" was, of course, the pursuit of spiritual reality through the all-surrounding material shadows. This pursuit left him no time for the ordinary comforts with which men console their loneliness. He was the eldest of six children, the son of a generous but bankrupt father and a loving but piously evangelical mother. He loved his family deeply and genuinely, but he was never completely at home within its circle. *Noli me tangere* was implicit in his attitude.

And so, despite his real love for his mother, he could not bear, even as a youth, any open display of familiar affection from her, and his love for his father was frequently spoiled by his pious disapproval of the elder Newman's loosely jovial and irresponsible personality. His progress was thus an unwilled but constant withdrawal from the sympathy of familial attachments.

At fifteen, young John Henry, preparing to leave school for a vacation at home, confided thoughts like the following to his journal: "In a few days I must go home. Then Satan will leap upon me with new though familiar enticements. Give me strength that I may defeat the world, the flesh, and the devil. Especially watch over me that I may not yield to the enticements of the world, lest drawn too much by its songs, dances and allurements I prefer these things to my God." Welcome home, young Newman! There seems little danger that you will ever sing or dance too much.

Newman was essentially "an emotional man dominated by his intelligence," O'Faolain believes, and this is probably a generally just appraisal of an amazingly complex man. Newman was not "cold." He loved and cared and suffered deeply all his life. But as his great intelligence became ever more exquisitely refined it tended more and more to limit the range of his emotional commitments. The great affections of his life were born of his intellectual and spiritual pilgrimage. Hurrell Froude and Ambrose St. John (the two human beings he love best), were both companions on his pilgrimage, and it was only with such fellow travelers that Newman could feel completely at ease. His family, unable to accompany him, grew ever dimmer, and the pilgrim himself seemed more lonely at each step.

Newman's youth and young manhood is treated with neither undue solemnity nor irreverent levity in this remarkable book. For all his great endowments of mind and soul, John Henry Newman was not always an easy man to love. He was certainly a genius and possibly a saint, but he was sometimes also an eccentric and, especially in his youth, an undeniable prig.

Sean O'Faolain succeeds in capturing a previously little known completeness in his study. He may add little to our knowledge of Newman's towering meaning in the spiritual and intellectual drama of our time, but he reveals with brilliance and sympathy the personal genesis of "that brave, kind, solitary, gifted, tormented angel" in whose mission many of his contemporaries, and many in our own generation, have so passionately believed.

The Poet in America

▬ It has been said that when W. H. Auden was asked why he had chosen to leave Europe in order to live in New York he answered that he had come to the great city in order to be alone. And Stephen Spender, in an essay published in this country several years ago, remarked that the "situation" of the American writer was one distinguished by its loneliness and isolation.

When all due allowances have been made for the limitations of a Whitmanesquely romantic view of America as a massive, extroverted monolith, magnificently contemptuous of the cloister and the academy, one must yet admit the true perception inherent in Auden's answer and Spender's observation. America's tradition has not been famous for its sympathy toward the artist and the intellectual. These very few words, in fact, still suggest something foreign and effete to some Americans. As a result, many of the nation's writers have felt a sense of alienation from the main currents of their country's life.

Thus alienated, frustrated in their attempts to communicate with others, America's writers have frequently been limited to talking to each other. The medium of their conversation has been the "little magazines," which have served in this country as a necessarily limited substitute for the more expansive and influential avenues of communication available in London and Paris. It has been in the "little magazines" that much of the freshly

Commonweal, 31 October 1952

creative, imaginative, and intellectual work of this century has been done by Americans. These magazines have thus served both to relieve the American writer's isolation and to provide an opportunity otherwise lacking for the discovery of unorthodox talent.

One of the most valuable of these magazines has been *Poetry*. Founded in 1912 by Harriet Monroe, this magazine has consistently published the work of unknown poets, and many of the poems it has published have remained as permanently valuable additions to the tradition of American letters. *Poetry* has provided two generations of American writers with an audience and a hope. And now, this October, it has published a special fortieth anniversary number, containing the work of some of America's most promising new poets.

Poetry's long and distinguished history reminds us of how important such independent magazines have been in our cultural life, and how necessary they will continue to be in a future which promises little relief from the overriding commercialization of American life. The writer in America may continue to be more isolated and alone than in other times and cultures, but with genuine encouragement he may create in the future even more fruitfully than he has in the past. And if this should happen, the forty-year history of *Poetry* indicates that, despite any isolation or alienation, the future of American verse may be very promising indeed.

François Mauriac

■ One of the basic dilemmas of the Christian artist and a perennial problem for Catholic criticism, was indicated by Cardinal Newman when, in his discourse on "Duties of the Church Toward Knowledge," he denied the possibility of there ever being a "Christian literature." His denial was based on what seemed to him a self-evident principle: you cannot have sinless literature of sinful man. If you attempt it, he warned, you may create something nobler than any literature ever was, but it will not be literature at all. Because literature must always be, not the vision of man as he should be, regenerate, but the record of man as he so tragically is, fallen from grace.

Perhaps no great writer in our century has felt this dilemma more cruelly or suffered its implications more publicly than the recipient of this year's Nobel prize in literature, M. François Mauriac. The ultimate recognition and eminence which have now been granted him in this award testify to his achievement in resolving it to the satisfaction of his own conscience and the approval of the world of letters.

On the one hand, Mauriac has, from his earliest years, been illumined by a faith which seemed to possess him wholly: "I belong to that race of people who, born in Catholicism, realize in earliest manhood that they will never be able to escape from it, will never be able to leave it or re-enter it. They were within it, they are within it, for ever and ever. They are inundated with light; they know that it is true."

On the other hand, Mauriac has, again from his earliest years, possessed a sensual imagination distinguished for its vividness, and an insight into the psychology of the sinner remarkable for its sensitivity and sympathy. The faith, the sensual imagination, and the psychology of sin have existed side by side in his works. As a result, some of the pious have been scandalized, a few of the sophisticated have been amused, and others, notably Mauriac himself, have been troubled.

Among the amused was André Gide, who, in a vein of distinguished malice, once wrote Mauriac concerning . . . "this reassuring compromise, which allows you to love God without losing sight of Mammon, causes you anguish of conscience and at the same time gives a great appeal to your face and great savor to your writings; and it ought to delight those who, while abhorring sin, would hate not to be able to give a lot of thought to it."

Mauriac's answer to Gide's taunt was *God and Mammon*, a prolonged examination of conscience likely to remain the most brilliant abstract resolution available of a problem concretely solved in Mauriac's novels. It is the problem, indicated by Newman, of the Christian artist's functioning in a medium which, of its very nature, holds grave dangers of a certain connivance with evil.

For Mauriac has created a "Christian literature" in the only sense that it can ever exist — a literature which treats of man as he indeed is, fallen, but which does not stop at the fact of the fall, but sees beyond to its infinite immensity and the possibility of its infinite redemption. The Christian artist, like any other artist, must look into the eyes of the sinner, but what should distinguish his gaze from the others is the compassion and the ultimate understanding with which he records what he has seen there.

Mauriac has looked deeper — deeper than some who have found his novels too knowledgeable of evil for their tastes care to look. But his vision of the sinner, however somber, has been redeemed by a more profound vision — the vision of the Cross, standing firm in the center of a world frequently unable to see it, which imparts the final meaning to his work. In that work the most vexing problems of the Christian artist are involved, and so, in the honor which has now crowned it, all Christian artists are indirectly honored. This great Frenchman has spoken for them all.

The Intuition of Jacques Maritain

"Art is the flower and perfection of this world." — Art and Poetry

■ There is paradox in the fact that the artist has come into his own in an age which hates him. The triumph of industrial civilization and of bourgeois culture has left the artist alienated from society, but, as André Malraux points out, it has also left him free. In exile from a hostile world he has discovered himself; unburdened of that world, he has turned inward and grown self-aware.

This discovery of himself, this increased self-awareness, has had a revolutionary effect on the artist's work. Modern poetry is distinguished by its intense longing for self-knowledge. "At such a time [as the present]," Jacques Maritain wrote in 1944, "poetry must work in two directions at once. It must continue to express itself creatively, and it must dwell introspectively on its own nature." The necessity of dwelling "on its own nature," he said, perhaps explains the unprecedented critical activity which has taken place in our age. This activity has eventually led modern poetry beyond techniques, beyond an analysis of meaning and of the meaning of meaning, to ask the first question, the ontological question: what *is* poetry? Its quest for self-discovery has brought it, finally, to the door of philosophy, to ask its own name.

Commonweal, 28 December 1953

Philosophy has not refused the question; the door has not been shut. In the work which he began in *Art and Scholasticism* and has now completed in *Creative Intuition in Art and Poetry*, Jacques Maritain has provided that ontology which was poetry's greatest need.

In his earlier work, *Art and Scholasticism*, Maritain seemed almost to apologize for writing on poetry at all. "The author," he said, "is only a philosopher. A philosopher's professional duty is to remain in the sky of metaphysics, the only enduring empyrean." *Art and Scholasticism* made obvious, however, that Maritain was not "only a philosopher" and that he could not "remain in the sky of metaphysics." Because here in the area of art – as elsewhere – his intense concern for the existential, his humanism and his charity, continually assert themselves. Maritain cannot be *only* the metaphysician; he must also be Maritain. And so he must be committed to *this* poem, to *this* society, to *this* person. He therefore writes on poetry as a philosopher who loves poetry, and he brings light from "the sky of metaphysics" to illumine the art of the ages.

Creative Intuition in Art and Poetry, for example, could not have been written by a man who was only a philosopher any more than it could have been by a man who was only an artist. The range of its poetic knowledge is as impressive as the brilliance of its metaphysical flights. It could have been written only by a philosopher-artist.

Maritain, like every good scholastic philosopher, begins by distinguishing his terms. Art and poetry, he says at the very beginning of *Creative Intuition*, cannot do without one another. Yet the two words are far from being synonymous. He explains:

By art I mean the creative or producing, word-making activity of the human mind. By poetry I mean, not the par-

ticular art which consists in writing verses, but a process
both more general and more primary: that intercommunication between the inner being of things and the inner being
of the human Self which is a kind of divination (as was realized in ancient times; the Latin *vates* was both a poet and a
diviner). Poetry, in this sense, is the secret life of each and
all the arts; another name for what Plato called *mousike.*

Poetry, then, is that which is an "intercommunication between
the inner being of things and the inner being of the human Self" —
and this whether it take the form of music, painting, or verse.

The starting point of Maritain's investigation is empirical: he
observes the development of painting from the art of the ancient Orient to the art of the modern West, and sees that art's
development has been from objectivity to subjectivity, from a
concern with Things to a concern with Self. Oriental art was
intent only on things; modern art is intent only on Self. The
progress of art has been the progress of individuality.

But, Maritain observes, at the very time art was most objective — most intent on Things — it revealed (almost against its
wishes) much of the artist's self, and at a time like the present,
when art is most subjective, it reveals (again, almost against
its wishes) the secret aspects of Things. What, he asks, does this
mean? What is the philosophical impact of this factual conclusion? He answers: "At the root of the creative act there must
be a quite particular intellectual process, without parallel in
logical reason, through which Things and the Self are grasped
together by means of a kind of experience or knowledge which
has no conceptual expression and is expressed only in the artist's work." Are we therefore to think, he asks, "that in such an
experience, creative in nature, Things are grasped in the Self
and the Self is grasped in Things, and subjectivity becomes a
means of catching obscurely the inner side of Things?"

Maritain's answer to this question is the major burden of his book. And his answer is: Yes. Poetry *is* a kind of knowledge which has no conceptual expression and through it subjectivity *does* become a means of catching obscurely the inner side of things. It is the means by which we recover that "denser and more refractory world" of which John Crowe Ransom has written—a world which cannot be known through scientific, discursive reason or through concepts, because it will not yield its secrets to them. These secrets, Maritain says, can be revealed only through poetry. They are caught in the earliest art known to man and they are explored throughout history by means of the artist's creative intuition. They are the hidden spiritual life of Things and of Self:

> Let us look at those deer and bison painted on the walls of prehistoric caves, with the admirable and infallible élan of virgin imagination. They are the prime achievement of human art and poetic intuition. By the virtue of Sign, they make present to us an aspect of the animal shape and life, and of the world of hunting. And they make present to us the spirit of those unknown men who drew them, they tell us that their makers were men, they reveal a Creative Self endowed with immortal intelligence, pursuing deliberately willed ends, and capable of sensing beauty.

And so, Maritain affirms, poetry is essentially a kind of knowledge. Having its roots in the preconscious life of the intellect, moved to expression by the poet's intuition of reality, given life in a work of art, poetry makes known something which was not known before and cannot be known in any other way: the spiritual world of an individual subjective experience.

Poetry is, as Maritain has said elsewhere, a "divination of the spiritual in the things of sense." The poet's vocation is thus a very lofty one, for "just as God makes created participations of His Being exist outside of himself, so the poet puts himself into what he makes, and by realizing in his work something which was not known before, he does in a human way something which is analogous to the creative activity of God."

To know a true poem — a Bach cantata, an El Greco painting, a Hopkins sonnet — is to know a world, for a true poem is a world. To enter it is to enter greatness; to explore it is to explore the sublime. Maritain quotes Blake's famous lines:

> To see a world in a grain of sand
> And a heaven in a wild flower.

This seeing, this intuition of the spiritual in the things of sense, is what we call poetry. Maritain's formulations of this concept have great beauty, for example: "That transient motion of a beloved hand — it exists an instant and will disappear forever, and only in the memory of angels will it be preserved above time. Poetic intuition catches it in passing, in a faint attempt to immortalize it in time. But poetic intuition does not stop at this given existent; it goes beyond, and definitely beyond. Precisely because it has no conceptualized object, it tends and extends to the infinite, it tends toward all the reality which is engaged in any singular existing Thing." Poetry, we might say, is the natural spiritual life of man.

Creative Intuition in Art and Poetry is, as Marshall McLuhan has said, impossible to review. Its wealth defies counting; its insights defy outlining. Like a poem, it must be known in itself. All one can do at second hand is indicate some of its major themes.

I recall reading a criticism of Maritain some years ago in, I think, *The Dublin Review*. The critic characterized him as "a rapture-intoxicated man." This description was, I think, not completely unjust. Maritain believes in rapture. He does not despise the Muse. He insists that in all great art the element of inspiration — in his phrase, of creative intuition — must be present. (The artist, he writes, is not an engineer.) And he tells us not to be "afraid" of the Romantics.

But Maritain is not himself a Romantic. He respects rapture but he is not, as his critic thought, intoxicated by it. He insists always upon the intellectual basis of art ("art is a virtue of the practical intellect") and he does not mistake poetic knowledge for absolute knowledge. In his aesthetics, as in all else, he is the integral humanist illumined by revelation. Nothing that is native to man is despised by him, but everything is ordered by wisdom.

The great and final achievement of *Creative Intuition and Poetry* is this ordering, this placing of art in the hierarchy of human values. Art, Maritain insists, is an activity both natural to man and necessary to his good. And so he vindicates art. Poetry is no dream. It is, ultimately, a level of reality, and the poet is he who intuits in his work what did not exist before his work, who gives to the world a knowledge of that which could not be known except for him. He is not an entertainer; he is not a propagandist; he is not an escapist; he is not a dreamer. He is a creator. And so too, certainly, is Jacques Maritain.

Frederick Baron Corvo's Hadrian the Seventh

■ In September 1913, Frederick Rolfe, alias Frederick Baron Corvo, destitute and dissolute in Venice, sent a last desperate appeal to one of his long-suffering, much abused benefactors in England: "My dear man: I'm in an awful state; and I firmly believe that I'm finished if I don't get relief *instanter*. . . . My dear man, I'm so awfully lonely. And tired. Is there no way of setting me straight?"

There was, tragically, no way. Rolfe's physical, moral, and artistic credit as well as his economic, was long since hopelessly exhausted. In October 1913, alone, insolvent, and embittered, he died in his Venetian rooming house. There were few who noticed, and to those who did it must have seemed that, at fifty-four, he had already lived too long.

But in the best romantic tradition that genius dead is more appreciated than genius living, Fredrick Rolfe's nagging misfortune has not followed him to the grave. He has been remembered and celebrated by a small but devout cult of admirers who have found in his extant works, especially the *Chronicles of the House of Borgia*, and *Hadrian the Seventh*, fare rich enough to excite the most exacting taste.

It was of *Hadrian the Seventh*, for example, that D. H. Lawrence wrote: "This book remains a clear and definite book of our epoch, not to be swept aside. If it is the book of a demon, as [Rolfe's] contemporaries said, it is a book of a man demon, not a mere poseur. And if some of it is caviare, it at least came out of the belly of a live fish." Now, reissued in a handsome new edition, it may at last receive the audience it deserves. For, although *Hadrian* can never be every man's book, it remains one of the most remarkable novels of this century, a *roman à clef* perhaps unparalleled for its special qualities of brilliantly opinionated insight, ironically self-critical apologia, and basically religious irreverence. Its hero, George Arthur Rose, declares: "As for the Faith, I found it comfortable. As for the Faithful, I found them intolerable." The story of his sudden and fantastic emergence from impoverished obscurity to the Supreme Pontificate of the Holy Roman Church is essentially the idealized autobiography of Rolfe himself. It is his terrible vengeance on the faithful — and his shy tribute to the faith.

Frederick Rolfe was the European "spoiled priest" *par excellence.* A convert to Catholicism, he studied briefly for the priesthood at the Scots' College in Rome. Then, expelled for what we can easily believe to have been obvious temperamental inadequacies, he spent his life nourishing both his longing for Holy Orders and his paranoiac resentment of those whose obduracy denied them to him. A grotesque combination of rococo temperament and Gothic facade, he seemed incapable of normally admirable human emotions. His constitutional inability to love or to be loved left him a tortured eccentric. A man of genius and longing, forever unrecognized and unsatisfied, he vented his wrath on all who came near him. But if the waste of greatness is the secret of tragedy, a part, at least, of the enduring significance of *Hadrian the Seventh* lies in its evidence of how much genius was wasted in the real life of Frederick Rolfe.

For *Hadrian the Seventh* is Frederick Rolfe's dream of what his life might, and one can be sure, in his view should, have been. It is his "If I Were Pope." And although we may be grateful that the seminary priests squelched whatever wild chance there ever was that a future Father Frederick Rolfe might someday actually reign as Hadrian the Seventh, we must yet sorrow that, as a result of their wisdom, so much was lost.

George Arthur Rose, in the Prooimion to *Hadrian the Seventh*, is spending one of his typical days: alone in his room, he intermittently broods, reads, writes, prays, talks to his cat, and counts the "split infinitives in the day's *Pall Mall Gazette*." Upon this scene enter two prelates, the "Bishop of Caerleon" and the aged "Cardinal-Archbishop of Pimlico." They have come to right an ancient wrong by begging George Arthur Rose to accept the Holy Orders long denied him. He condescendingly accepts their offer of immediate ordination, but only after they promise to pay off all his creditors themselves.

Soon afterward, through a chain of wildly implausible circumstances made somehow credible by Rolfe, the much wronged Mr. Rose is elected to the See of Peter. He immediately establishes the flavor of his reign:

> They brought Him before the altar, and set Him in a crimson velvet chair, asking what Pontifical name He would choose.
>
> "Hadrian the Seventh"; the response came unhesitatingly, undemonstratively.
>
> "Your Holiness would perhaps prefer to be called Leo, or Pius, or Gregory, as is the modern manner?" the Cardinal-Dean inquired with imperious suavity.
>
> "The previous English Pontiff was Hadrian the Fourth; the present English Pontiff is Hadrian the Seventh. It pleases Us; and so, by Our Own Impulse, We command."

The irrepressible and enigmatic Hadrian then proceeds, during a short reign, to remake the Church—and the world. He encounters, not unnaturally, some opposition, but all eventually yields before his learning, wisdom, subtlety, and strength. He creates most of his friends cardinals (thus "packing" the Sacred College). He sells the temporal treasures of the Church and distributes their proceeds to the poor. He humbles the proud Jesuits, and exalts the lowly Franciscans. He renounces the Church's claim to temporal sovereignty.

Cardinal Ragna, his archenemy, threatens to denounce him as "pseudopontiff and heretic" because of all this, but even the wily Ragna must finally cower before Hadrian's superiority. Hadrian denounces "Socialism" and the hated myth of "equality" and, as the acknowledged Father of Kings and Princes, restores the full glory of the Holy Roman Empire. Finally, while walking in procession through the streets of Rome, supported on one side by the Northern Emperor and on the other by the Southern, he is shot by a Socialist fanatic.

> The Apostle raised Himself a little, supported by imperial hands. How bright the sunlight was, on the warm grey stones, on the ripe Roman skins, on vermillion and lavender and blue and ermine and green and gold, on the indecent grotesque blackness of two blotches, on apostolic whiteness and the rose of blood.

Hadrian intoned his Apostolic Blessing for the city and the world, then:

> The hand and the dark eyelashes drooped and fell. The delicate fastidious lips closed, in the ineffable smile of the dead who have found the Secret of Love, and are perfectly satisfied.
>
> So died Hadrian the Seventh, Bishop, Servant of the servants of God, and (some say) Martyr. So died Peter in the arms of Caesar.
>
> The world sobbed, sighed, wiped its mouth, and experienced extreme relief.

Ignazio Silone's A Handful of Blackberries

━━ In 1927 Ignazio Silone and Palmiro Togliatti went to Moscow as the Italian representatives at a special session of the Communist International. Silone was disillusioned, sick, at what he learned there. Afterward, in Switzerland, Togliatti tried to reassure him: "The forms of Proletarian Revolution were not arbitrary," Togliatti argued. "If they did not accord with our prejudices, so much the worse for us." Silone's reply to his friend was not very coherent, he says, "mainly because Togliatti's arguments were purely political, whereas the agitation which my recent experiences aroused in me went far beyond politics."

Silone's agitations (and they have been many) have all gone beyond politics, beyond abstractions, and beyond ideologies to reach his ultimate and perhaps only concern, which is "the superiority of the human person over all the economic and social mechanisms which oppress him." And as the years have gone by, Silone tells us, there has been added to this concern "an intuition of man's dignity and a feeling of reverence for that which in man is always trying to outdistance itself, and lies at the root of his eternal disquiet."

The human person; man's dignity; reverence; eternal disquiet: these things brought the young Silone into the Party and led the matured Silone out of it; they are the basis of his present Socialism, and they are the distinction of his art. Eliot has reminded us that we can apply only literary criteria to determine whether a work is "literature" but that to determine its *greatness* as literature we must apply other tests — ethical, philosophical, theological. Silone's novels, like his politics, go beyond their genre. They are informed by his ultimate concern and his added intuition. They are great art because they go beyond "art."

A key to all of them is provided in Silone's observation on an earthquake which destroyed a large part of his province and killed about fifty thousand of its people in 1915: "I was surprised," he has written, "to see how much my fellow-villagers took this appalling catastrophe as a matter of course. The geologists' complicated explanations, reported in the newspapers, aroused their contempt. In a district like ours, where so many injustices go unpunished, people regarded the recurrent earthquakes as a phenomenon requiring no further explanation. In fact, it was astonishing that earthquakes were not more frequent. An earthquake buries rich and poor, learned and illiterate, authorities and subjects alike beneath its ruined houses. . . . An earthquake achieves what the law promises but does not in practice maintain — the equality of all men."

The hero of Silone's novels is always this Italian peasant, unterrified by earthquakes, and their setting is always this Abbruzean village; in them he finds a universal theme: man's fortitude — extended to stoicism — in the face of suffering, and man's thirst after justice, his "eternal disquiet."

In *A Handful of Blackberries* the Fascists are gone from the village and the Communists have taken their place. The gramophone in the public square which used to play "Giovinezza" now blares forth "The Internationale." Many things which were crimes under the old regime have now become virtues. But the peasant is not surprised at all this. Earthquakes come and go; his valley remains. He plows the fields, sweats in the heat, is numb with cold, loves, and begets children — and waits.

A Handful of Blackberries tells the story of the coming of the Party to Silone's valley in 1946. It is concerned, in its story line, with a young engineer, Rocco de Donatis, and his sweetheart, Stella. Rocco, thirsting for justice, had become a Communist in his youth. Stella, for the same reason, had become one too. They meet when Rocco comes to the valley to organize the peasants and suppress deviations from the Party line. But, shortly after his coming, Rocco is sent to Russia. He then *sees* the Revolution. And so it is only a question of time before his native decency triumphs over his ideological regularity. (For what agitates him is "beyond politics.") When he returns to the valley he breaks with the Party. The bulk of the story concerns his and Stella's struggles as the Party attempts to ruin them.

This looks, on the surface, like a "political novel." But I don't think that the political label fits it, except in a very special sense. The politics are almost accidental to Silone's real concern. "On a group of theories one can found a school," he has said, "but on a group of values one can found a culture, a civilization, a new way of living together among men." His concern here, as always, is with values as they inhere in the peasant life of which he writes. They are pagan values, in the proper, classical sense, and for them Silone feels a classical piety. His work is a twentieth-century version of pastoral. It celebrates, and reverences, life at its most enduring roots. Politics? Theories? History? What are these in the face of the mystery of life and death, and of man's endurance in meeting it?

There is an ancient trumpet in the valley, used only to call the peasants together when some great wrong has been done them. This trumpet is the perpetual fear of their oppressors and must be kept hidden. At the end of *A Handful of Blackberries* it has been hidden from the Communists — and lost.

"Can't it ever be found again?" Stella asks the trumpeter. "How can I know?" he replies. "It doesn't depend on me, you

Graham Greene's The Quiet American

▬ Graham Greene, it should by now be universally acknowledged, has one of the cleanest, most pointed prose styles, of any
novelist now writing in English. It should be acknowledged too
that as a master of the narrative technique — as an arranger of
time, a manipulator of detail and conjurer of atmosphere — his
position is preeminent. The publication of *The Quiet American*
calls for a third acknowledgment: Mr. Greene, in spite of the
illusion of realism his work imparts, is primarily, and inveter-
ately, a moralist. Behind his art there always lurks a parable.
When the chips are down, at moments of crisis, his characters
speak a language that can be learned only in the Greene Theological School.

One of course suspected this before, and some of Mr. Greene's
admirers, including myself, were dismayed by it. *The Heart of
the Matter* raised some uneasy questions about what "religion"
might be doing to Mr. Greene's talents, and *The End of the Affair*, with its (for many of us) intolerable retreat to the pseudo-
miraculous, gave the questions an unhappy answer.

Now, we are told, Mr. Greene has put aside supernatural
themes to write a series of "nonreligious" novels, of which *The
Quiet American* is the first. It may be, but only superficially.
Priests and confessionals are absent from its Indochinese setting, but it tortures over the same moral problems as did Mr.

Commonweal, 16 March 1956

Greene's earlier works. This book may speak with a secular accent, but its meaning is not limited to this world. Its narrator, the English journalist Fowler, does not believe in God, but he talks about Him a good deal of the time, and at the very end of the story, after the sins have been irreparably committed, he complains: "How I wish there existed someone to whom I could say that I was sorry."

Fowler, like all the characters in Mr. Greene's world, has a besetting sin. Selfishness. "I know myself," he says, "and I know the depth of my selfishness." But like any besetting sin in Mr. Greene's world, Fowler's selfishness takes unusual, complex turns: "I cannot be at ease (and to be at ease is my chief wish) if someone else is in pain. . . . Sometimes this is mistaken by the innocent for unselfishness, when all I am doing is sacrificing a small good [his immediate convenience] for the sake of a far greater good — a peace of mind — when I need think only of myself."

One of the "innocent" who so mistakes it is Alden Pyle, the "quiet American" of Mr. Greene's title. Pyle is a young American, fresh from Harvard, who comes to Indochina as a member of the U.S. Economic Aid Mission. And Pyle is an idealist. He wants to "fight for liberty." When Fowler first meets him he thinks: "Perhaps only ten days ago he had been walking across the Common in Boston, his arms full of books he had been reading in advance on the Far East and the problems of China. . . . He was absorbed already in the dilemmas of democracy and the responsibilities of the West; he was determined — I learned that very soon — to do good, not to any individual person, but to a country, a continent, a world. Well, he was in his element now, with the whole universe to improve."

For Fowler, such innocence is sentimental cant. *He* knows that the world cannot be "improved," that words like "democracy" and "honor" are mere traps to catch the unsophisticated. He is a reporter for a British paper and he writes of what he sees. But he is not engagé. Opium he finds comforting, and his mistress. Abstractions and ideals are for fools, uninitiates, the Pyles of the world.

That was Pyle's trouble: his abstract ideals, learned from some textbook. He had some notion about creating a Third Force in Indochina, and this led him to supply explosives to terrorists who, he hoped, would take over the country and set up a government on whom the United States could rely. The consequences of his meddling were disastrously bloody, and in the end there was no way out but to get rid of him. Fowler, to this end, connived in his murder. (As a result of the murder he got back the mistress whom Pyle — a rank amateur at illicit love — had temporarily lured away with naive American talk about children, home, and nation.)

Mr. Greene has written a parable of Americans abroad and, one might legitimately complain, his parable has faults that moralistic tales inevitably suffer from. Alden Pyle is a caricature, a mere foil for Fowler's — or Mr. Greene's — chagrin. Well-intentioned and stupid ("he was impregnably armored by his good intentions and his ignorance," Fowler observes), he can cause nothing but trouble wherever he happens to meddle, whether it be in politics or love. It is not on a political level, however, that *The Quiet American* has significance. Its parable is deeper than politics — or geography. As in all of Mr. Greene's novels, it concerns the moral life. Pyle, the innocent, dangerous American, and Fowler, the sophisticated, safe Englishman, represent, behind the polish of Mr. Greene's art, the vices and virtues of a morality play.

And it is here that Mr. Greene finally fails, as I believe he finally failed in *The Heart of the Matter* and *The End of the Affair*. The work does not come to terms with its own burden. It takes refuge in easy ways out. Pyle and Fowler, on a certain level are brilliantly conceived, brilliantly executed. But this is not the level for which Mr. Greene is reaching — the lofty level of innocence, suffering and death. On this level they are not at home, nor could they be. They have no meaning in the Dostoevskian universe that Mr. Greene would probably like to create. They are, rather, mere mouthpieces for certain ideas constant in Mr. Greene's work. They interest us and amuse us and even, at times, move us. But they do not, in any ultimate sense, illuminate the darkness that Mr. Greene sees everywhere about.

Arnold Toynbee's Christianity Among the Religions of the World

— In this as in his last book (*An Historian's View of Religion*), Professor Toynbee plays the role of synthesist: surveying the vast, complex area of the traditional higher religions, he attempts to indicate what the future of these religions, acting together in a civilization that is struggling to be born, will be. And if Professor Toynbee as historian was, in some circles, a cause for controversy, Professor Toynbee as theologian seems likely, in other circles, to be cause for despair.

Whatever despair is felt, however, will not be over Professor Toynbee's intentions: they are manifestly good. Nor, for that matter, will it be over his insights: many of them are brilliant. It will be felt, rather, over the theological-philosophical hodge-podge that somehow emerges from the two.

Professor Toynbee's basic insight is a profound one: in modern history a new and terrible phenomenon has arisen, the phenomenon of a totalitarian materialism that takes the form of Nationalism and Communism. The root of this materialism is man's worship of himself. In the face of this, the great religions of the world, forgetting their ancient rancors, must stand together to vindicate their common vision of man.

Few reasonably enlightened theologians would oppose Professor Toynbee here. Where Professor Toynbee falls from insight to sentimentality is in his specific recommendations.

In his recommendations for Christianity, for example, Professor Toynbee says that "we ought . . . to try to purge our Christianity of the traditional Christian belief that Christianity is unique." He admits that this will be difficult, but it must be done, he says, if we are to purge Christianity of "exclusive-mindedness and intolerance."

The essence of the Christian religion *is* its conviction of its own uniqueness. The Christ has come. In its efforts, however well-intentioned, to explain that uniqueness away, Professor Toynbee's book seems a curious return to the banalities of an eighteenth-century kind of rationalism.

Christianity and the New Age

How the Church should confront the world is a problem as old as the Church itself. Jesus (who, the Church confesses, is the Christ) warned his disciples that the world would hate and persecute them, and the world of imperial Rome justified his warning. But the Christian sect survived the Caesars, and upon the ruins of their power it fashioned a high civilization, the twilight of which has descended only today.

In this twilight Christianity again must ask the question: how should the Church confront the world? And it must ask with an urgency the Church has not felt for almost fifteen hundred years. Because, although the future is uncertain, some present things are clear. The old religious-humanist order is passing and a new technological-secularist order is emerging. Whatever was the role of Christianity in a civilization it helped to create, its role will be radically different in a civilization from whose birth it has been absent. For religion, the securities it knew for centuries are probably forever past. The implications of this fact, both for religion and for society, are tremendous.

In recent books two theologians — one a Roman Catholic, the other an Evangelical Protestant — deal with these implications. Both men are distinguished. Both write with a profound knowledge of, and a passionate concern for, the tensions emerging between Christianity and a new age. Both realize the pathetic inadequacy of a comfortable "bourgeois" Christianity for resolving the tensions. Both deal, specifically, with the historically unprecedented challenge Christianity faces from Communism. And, on almost every point, the two men reach radically different conclusions. In these two books we see, perhaps, divisions that will torture the Christian mind as it grapples anew with the problem of the Church and the world.

Father [Martin C.] D'Arcy's *Communism and Christianity* is in the great tradition of Catholic intellectualism. The distinguished English Jesuit is a humanist philosopher as well as a theologian, and his book has virtues that one too seldom finds in religious writing on Marxism. There is no stridency here; D'Arcy recognizes, and brilliantly analyzes, Marxism for what it is: a pseudo "religion" which, for all its perversity, is rooted in a legitimate demand for justice and order. Communism is so dangerous precisely because, more than most systems, it approaches a vision of humanity that satisfies fundamental cravings of the human spirit. What is demonic in Communism is that it takes a partial truth and seeks to make it the whole.

To this partial, perverted truth, D'Arcy opposes the total Christian vision, which, he insists, alone encompasses man. If the civilization to come is to be more than an ant-civilization, this vision must be vindicated within it. Like Léon Bloy, Martin D'Arcy would agree that "religion," historically, has often been religion's worst enemy. ("The Lord Jesus," Bloy acidly commented, "is very decorative in shop windows.") "Righteousness" has been made a mask for complacency and the "Christian" order was too often a guarantor of social inequity. Out of these things the secular utopianism of Marxism was born.

But, D'Arcy insists, between the eschatology of Christianity and the eschatology of Communism there stands an insurmountable wall. In the final analysis, the former means freedom, the latter slavery for man. To the false messianism of Marxism, of any other secularism which reduces man to a thing, Christianity must proclaim the true Messiah, the Christ. In whatever world it finds itself, this is the Church's mission to the end of days.

"What Christianity and Communism have to offer," D'Arcy concludes, "are then as different as heaven from earth, and it would appear that they must meet in a head-on collision; and they both are concerned with the welfare of man and can look as if they were brothers. . . . [But] the two cannot live in the same world." (One feels obliged to note that the general excellence of *Communism and Christianity* is marred by the curious "Preface to the American Edition" which it now carries. It is difficult to believe that the M. C. D'Arcy who signed this preface is the same Martin D'Arcy who wrote the book. The spirit of the preface — with its simple-minded view of Communism as a cloak-and-dagger conspiracy — violates practically everything the book's text so judiciously establishes. What sea-change, one wonders, could make this Oxford don sound, in his "American" preface, like a propagandist for the late Senator McCarthy?)

If Father D'Arcy's book is in the tradition of Catholic intellectualism, Professor [Joseph L.] Hromadka's work is in the tradition of Protestant prophecy. D'Arcy analyzes, distinguishes; the Czech theologian proclaims. What he proclaims is that the old order of Western bourgeois civilization is already dead and stinking. The new order is upon us; the age of the proletarian revolution has come. And the Christian affirmation, if it is to be made at all, must be made in a language this age can understand: the Church, with whatever reservations, must come to terms with Marx. "What is needed," he writes, "is a . . . realization that — humanly speaking — the future of the Christian Church and theology depends on our courage to take the revolutionary changes in the east of Europe and in Asia as an opportunity to an "ideology." But the Word is not without meaning for the temporal affairs of men, and there are some things to which it must say no. It is the *no* established by D'Arcy, in terms both of religion and of man, that provides the necessary corrective to Hromadka's work.

Walter Lippmann's
The Communist World and Ours

▬ Almost fifty years ago, Walter Lippmann studied at Harvard under George Santayana. In the subsequent decades Lippmann has played many roles: diplomat, editor, moralist, journalist, pundit par excellence. In all of them one can see traces of the Santayana spirit. While the century has grown progressively anarchic, Lippmann has been a public monument to the life of reason. To a generation caught up in fanaticisms and crusades he has proclaimed a sense of contingency, irony, tradition, and that ordered skepticism about history which (in Santayana's view) is the mark of a civilized man.

The Communist World and Ours, Mr. Lippmann's report on his conversations last autumn with Premier Khrushchev, exemplifies this balanced reasonableness, which has been the author's major contribution to our public life. Here, as elsewhere, he attempts to bring a measure of objectivity and detachment to a problem that is usually clouded over with emotion and bombast. Mr. Lippmann is an enemy of illusions, and both East and West, he believes, are beset with them. He would have both reexamine the world coolly and be willing to settle for much less than either desires — because much less is all either can have if there is to be any future at all.

Worldview, April 1959

The views of both camps, Mr. Lippmann believes, are "derived from the same very human and common fallacy. It is the fallacy of assuming that this is one world and that the social order to which one belongs must either perish or become the universal order of mankind. "But," he says, "looking at the history of the globe, the truth, as I see it, is that there has never been one world. . . . The failure to recognize this truth that there are many worlds, not merely one, is, I believe, the deepest sort of confusion between us, and the most stubborn obstacle to that mutual toleration which is the very best that is conceivable between our two societies."

What Americans must do, Mr. Lippmann insists, is be rid of one-world illusions and "relax their fears in order to fortify and clarify their purposes." What their purposes must be, he thinks, are the nurturing and fortification of freedom in those areas of the world — Asia and Africa — where the real issue between democracy and totalitarianism will be resolved. Unless a heroic effort is made here, the future will indeed belong to Marxism.

"The Communists are expanding in Asia," he writes, "because they are demonstrating a way, at present the only obvious and effective way, of raising quickly the power and the standard of living of a backward people. The only convincing answer to that must be a demonstration by the non-Communist nations that there is another and more humane way of overcoming the immemorial poverty and weakness of the Asian peoples.

"This demonstration can be best made in India," Mr. Lippmann says, "and there is little doubt in my mind that if we and our Western partners could underwrite and assure the success of India's development, it would make a world of difference. It might be decisive in turning the tide. It would put an end to the enervating feeling of fatality and inevitability, to the sense that Communism is the only wave of the future . . . and that

Evelyn Waugh's Monsignor Ronald Knox

— Evelyn Waugh has carefully defined both the limits and the
tone of his biography of Ronald Knox. In his preface he writes
that the primary purpose of his book "is to tell the story of
[Knox's] exterior life; not to give a conspectus of his thought;
still less to measure his spiritual achievements." And Mr. Waugh
tells us that if the picture he has drawn seems somber, it is, in-
tentionally so. The popular image of Ronald Knox is of a "cherished and privileged survivor of a golden age." But he writes,
"genius and sanctity do not thrive except by suffering. If I have
made too much of Ronald's tribulations, it is because he hid
them, and they must be known to anyone who seeks to appraise
his achievement."

Mr. Waugh's picture is indeed somber. It escapes being tragic
only because Ronald Knox himself would have scorned the notion of a "tragic destiny." Knox was not a Newman nor was he
meant to be. Parallels between the careers of the two converts
are obvious but superficial. Both intellectually and psychologically, they are worlds apart. Everyone — undergraduates fresh
at Oxford, remote acquaintances, the little children of friends —
called Knox "Ronnie." Newman could not have been called
"Johnnie" — even by Hurrell Froude himself.

Ronald Knox was, in the words of Mr. Waugh's preface, "the
brilliantly precocious youth, cosseted from childhood; the wit

and scholar marked out for popularity and fame; the boon companion of a generation of legendary heroes." He was the son of an Anglican bishop; he made a brilliant success at Oxford, and at twenty-four was ordained to the Anglican priesthood and elected a fellow and chaplain of Trinity College. At Trinity, he consolidated his early fame and developed his own cult, the members of which were, like himself, advanced Anglo-Catholics. But by 1917 he had decided to submit to Rome.

Shortly before his submission, his father, the bishop of Manchester, told Ronald: "Honestly I look upon the Roman priesthood as the grave of the talent that is especially yours." Like Newman's friends at Oxford seventy-five years before, Knox's friends in 1917 could see nothing but frustration and heartbreak in a decision to forsake the promise of his Anglican vocation for the uncertainties of an "alien" creed. But Knox was convinced and, with little of the public fanfare that marked Newman's conversion in 1845, he was received into the Church of Rome. Two years later he was ordained a Catholic priest.

The section on Knox's conversion occurs in the middle of Mr. Waugh's biography. By the time we reach it both the advantages and the disadvantages of Mr. Waugh's biographical method are clear. We have been treated to a wonderful evocation of Ronald Knox's golden youth and the golden generation of youths that make Oxford pathetically memorable before the end of all of these things in the Armageddon of 1914. But in this evocation — in the rigidly enforced externality of Mr. Waugh's treatment — something essential of Knox is lost. He was not a dilettante but in this biography, especially in the first half of it, he emerges as the dilettante par excellence.

All the ecclesiastical naughtiness, the ritualistic fun and games of a certain "advanced" Anglo-Catholicism are here, but there is no hint of any struggle with the high seriousness of a genuine Anglican tradition. Ronald and his friends had a wonderful time for a while trying to make their corner of the established church more Roman than Westminster Cathedral. They wore Italian-style surplices and collected rococo religious art; they delighted in scandalizing the Anglican moderates; but there is a remarkable absence of theology in their struggles; in these pages one is left with a suspicion that the Anglican crisis of Knox and his young circle was at least as aesthetic as it was intellectual.

The advantages and disadvantages of Mr. Waugh's method are equally apparent in the second, "Roman" half of the biography. But here the absence of serious attention to Knox's intellectual and spiritual history is not balanced by the external charm of an Oxford youth. We have, rather, the record of an almost too literal fulfillment of the bishop of Manchester's prophecy about the Roman priesthood's being the grave of his son's talent.

Since Newman it has been a legend in England that the Church does not know how to treat its most brilliant converts; certainly the legend, in Mr. Waugh's treatment at least, seems proved in the Catholic career of Ronald Knox. Knox himself recalled it when he was given great trouble by some members of the hierarchy over his translation of the scriptures. He wrote, in a letter, that because of this it would be said that "the Church of Rome does not want converts, finds them an embarrassment and does not know what to do with them."

The history of Knox's chaplaincy at Oxford is the history mostly of dull teas and dispirited dinners given by the chaplain for unwilling undergraduates. Knox wrote, of course, and preached; he did both brilliantly and his wit remained famous. And his translation of the Old and New Testaments would be a historic achievement in any age.

But in this book an awful pall of sadness hangs over every triumph. *Cui bono?* is the question that seems to haunt every chapter. Through it all one has a sense of something missed,

In Memoriam: H. A. R.
Preached at the Funeral
of Father H. A. Reinhold

■ We come here today in faith, in hope, and in love to celebrate the death of a Christian who was our friend, our brother,
and our dear father and teacher in God. We celebrate the victory of Jesus Christ in this priest, this brother, this father and
teacher. We have heard mighty words from the fifteenth chapter of 1 Corinthians and the seventeenth chapter of John — words
of resurrection and glory. We have heard the unimaginable and
unthinkable promises spoken to us by Paul and Jesus the Lord —
promises of victory over sin and death, of glory and life ever-
lasting. Now we must meditate upon these things.

It is fitting that we meditate in terms of the life and the teaching of this man, our friend and father, in whom Christ had
the victory. Because what we celebrate here today is not a private victory. It is not a life hidden with Christ in God that
we recall. All of our lives, in their deepest recesses, in those
innermost parts of our being that no man but God alone can
know, are hidden with Christ in God. God alone knows these
things and we leave them to God. What we celebrate here
today and give thanks for is a public life, a public ministry,
and a public example — a life, a ministry, and an example that

Worship, March 1968

taught many in our generation and will teach many in the generations to come.

But we come here today not only to celebrate a victory; many of us come also to pay a debt — the greatest of all debts, the debt of faith itself. Because Hans Ansgar Reinhold taught us (some of us when we were very young, some of us when we were older) to see in a way we had not seen before, in a way we had not suspected was possible before we had read him or knew him. He taught us to see the very things we celebrate today — the mystery and the joy of the church, that is, the mystery and joy of the resurrection and the glory of Christ Jesus.

The words of scripture we have heard and the meditation we now make are thus peculiarly appropriate for the burial rites of this Christian. Because resurrection and glory, the glory which the Son had with the Father before the world began and which is now appropriated to us through the Son's victory, are keys to the whole life and work of H. A. Reinhold. "We are resurrection men and alleluia is our song," Augustine told us. John Henry Newman also reminded us that ours is a resurrection religion — a religion of victory and vanquishment, of hope and light. Father Reinhold helped us to know this. His own life was a kind of perpetual Easter vigil. It was a recurrent passage from darkness to light. His witness was an affirmation of the centrality of Jesus Christ, the alpha and omega — the beginning and the end — our life even in death.

The resurrection victory of Jesus Christ was the foundation of Father Reinhold's love for the liturgy. Before others understood, he understood how the victory of the Lord is given to us in the celebration of his mysteries, and he knew that we must seek to communicate these mysteries through the liturgy's signs. We must remember today, however, that for Father Reinhold the mystery remained tremendous, after all the explanations had been made — the *mysterium tremendum*. This man, all of us who knew him know, was an enemy to superficiality: he was an enemy to mere aestheticism or to any easy popularism in the liturgy. He was plunged deep into the numinous; he was seized by the idea of the Holy. He knew that our best liturgies, like our best theologies, attempt by sign and analogy to speak what is finally unspeakable, to communicate what is ultimately uncommunicable. But he struggled through his life to make the signs of the mystery visible, and so to make it possible for us to enter with joy and thanksgiving into the celebration of the victory which Jesus Christ has begun and we are called, until the end of time, to complete.

Hans Reinhold was the enemy also of any approach to the Church or its liturgy which would reduce them to a kind of secular communitarianism. Nothing human was strange to him, but in its midst he affirmed the transcendent. He knew that we live in two orders; that in our travail, our suffering, our doubt, and our fear, in the shadow of death and defeat, we are even now sharers in a glory that is not ours, but is given to us as pure gift. As a man whose vision was a resurrection vision, he passionately, deeply, and forever loved the Church. He could not and would not separate the glory of Jesus Christ from the community and the custodian of that glory, the historic Church. He was a minister of mysteries that had been told to him by that Church. But he also knew how tragically the mystery of the Church can be obscured. He knew what Baron Friedrich von Hügel meant when he wrote (in another time and place, at the beginning of this century but perhaps not so long ago) that the faults of a certain kind of churchman are *sui generis,* and such that they destroy for many that vision of the mystery of the Church which alone makes life in the Church tolerable — and not only tolerable but the only life possible for us, for which there is no alternative.

Father Reinhold knew the pain of history. He knew what Paul

meant in the eighth chapter of Romans when, telling us of our glory, he tells us all that until the end of time all creation must wait, groaning, for the final revelation of God. Until then we must wait in hope. Without a sense of both history and theology man must be impatient. He must be angry. But Hans Reinhold had a deep sense of history and of theology, and he was infinitely patient. He transcended anger. He lived in hope.

Because of this, he did not finally fear. All of us who knew him may recall times when he seemed to fear. (He was a man some thought inordinately sensitive. He was a man much given to worry.) And at times Father Reinhold surely feared for himself. But he never feared for mankind. He never feared for the Church. He never confused his personal misfortunes and defeats with defeats for man. He never confused them with defeats for the Church.

Though he knew we must learn eschatological patience, Father Reinhold also knew that we are called to seek God's justice and show God's mercy in our own time and place. And here he was not patient. He was a man who by temperament was endowed with a love for freedom. He was a free spirit. He was formed in a humane and classical tradition, the tradition of an educated North German middle class, and this helped give him that independence and perspective which shaped all his judgments. But his natural gifts were transfigured by the light of the gospel. He knew with what marvelous dignity man was endowed in creation; he knew also, and even more deeply, with what greater dignity he was reformed in the incarnation. Father Reinhold had, I think, an intuition for justice. He felt that thirst after justice of which our Lord speaks. Who suffered and he did not suffer? Who wept and he did not weep? Who laughed and he did not laugh?

All of us who knew him know examples of these things. Before anyone else in the country was concerned over the plight of the migrant workers, Hans Reinhold suffered over the plight of the migrant workers. He suffered for the Jews. He suffered for the refugees. And his was not a mere intellectual suffering. This man was deeply troubled by the sufferings of man. No matter how wisely in any particular event, he involved himself always in causes which gave some practical expression to his concerns. He knew that Jesus Christ must be sought out and served in his brothers, in his lonely and suffering brothers, throughout all human history.

And so, finally, H. A. Reinhold had a passion for unity. He hated nationalism and longed for an international order. But, even more to our point, he longed for the unity of those who believe in Jesus Christ, who share his hope because they are marked already with his sign. For ecumenism as for the liturgy, Father Reinhold was a mighty prophet.

This man, I think, accomplished in himself St. Paul's command: "Fill your mind with everything that is good. Fill your mind with everything that is pure, everything that is worthy of love and respect, everything that is worthy of praise," Take these, cherish them, serve them.

And proclaim them. Proclaim them in the resurrection and the glory and hope of the Lord. Father Hans Reinhold proclaimed them. This is the cause of our joy today. This is the victory we celebrate in his death. The victory was given him and is given us in the same Christ, in the same gospel, and in the same Church. So, my dear brothers, let us give thanks to God, for giving us this hope, this victory, this glory, through Jesus Christ. Amen.

Sacerdos et Pontifex

━ John Joseph Wright, bishop, cardinal of the Holy Roman Church, who died in Boston on August 10, once told me about a Collect he especially loved, and about his feelings when he first prayed it at Mass in Rome soon after his ordination.

This Collect for the Third Sunday after Pentecost in the old missal (and now, like so many other profound and beautiful things, lost or strangely altered in the new missal) beseeched God, without whom nothing is strong, nothing is holy, to multiply his mercy upon us, so that with him for our ruler and guide, we may so pass through the good things of time that we do not lose those things which are eternal. John Wright's love of these words, and his reaction to them on a morning early in his priesthood, tell us much about this brilliant, complex, unforgettable man: intellectual, humanist, raconteur, friend, churchman, lover of the good things of this world *and* the glorious things of the world to come.

I can hear his wonderful voice, recalling the Collect and the Mass: "Think of the meaning of these words, *Sic transeamus per bona temporalia; ut non amittamus aeterna!*" Here, he said, the secret of Christian humanism was revealed to him. He prayed the Collect in an ancient Roman chapel, and as he prayed the sun streamed upon the marble altar where he stood. He felt at once — and all together — the splendor and the wonder and the

REVIEWS AND REFLECTIONS 141

joy of life: the pathos of its passing and the glory beyond the passing. He wept (as he often did), rejoicing, and went on with what he had to do.

John Wright loved the world. He loved his friends. He loved ideas and conversation, good food and good wine. Above all else, as he confessed, he loved the Church — one, holy, Catholic, apostolic, and, of course, *Roman*. The Church was the sign of those things which are eternal, set down among the good things, and the bad things, that pass. Who wounded (or seemed to wound) the Church wounded him. Who made the Church weep made him weep.

John Wright was a liberal Catholic in the tradition of French, English, and American liberal Catholicism, the tradition of Lacordaire, Dupanloup, Blondel and Maritain, Newman and Acton, Orestes Brownson, Archbishop Ireland, and *Commonweal* itself. Liberal Catholicism, in its nineteenth- and twentieth-century versions, existed in a state of tension between the prevailing Catholic ethos and the values of the "modern" world. It sought to reverse the popular Catholic distrust of many liberal values, to gain a wider, deeper acceptance among Catholics for the ideals of democracy, political and cultural pluralism, social and economic justice, intellectual freedom and diversity; it fought, and indeed abhorred, the authoritarian methods and mentalities which continued, until Vatican II at least, to earn the Church its reputation as a monolith. At the same time, liberal Catholicism opposed the dogmatic secularism and moral relativism that characterized much liberal thought. In and through all of this, liberal Catholicism prided itself on its fidelity to *basic* Catholic doctrines, on its love for and loyalty to the Church.

In 1952 I wrote an article in *Commonweal* called "The Liberal Catholic." In it I said that we liberal Catholics asked a radical revaluation among many of our fellow Catholics of their basic attitudes (mostly illiberal) towards the modern world. "This revaluation," I wrote, "demands no sacrifice of whatever is essential to the faith; it implies no surrender to relativism or secularism. Rather, it emphasizes the Church's genius for eternal renewal."

How dated this may now sound, a quarter century later. "The essentials of the faith" are not as clear as they seemed then. Certainly, for most, they are not as many. But to all who, with any intellectual honesty, continue to call themselves Catholic, there were, are, and always will be essentials. To affirm this proposition, to fight for it when many seem to think that the history of dogma, liturgy, and the Church itself began around 1966, is not to have become "conservative." It is to have survived, as a liberal Catholic, into an age when that center which *is* liberal Catholicism is threatened by attacks from right and left.

John Cardinal Wright did not leave the classic liberal Catholic tradition; it left him, or at least it disappeared as he had known it in the years and the angers that followed Vatican II; and he often seemed unable to distinguish between what was substantial and what was foolish and fashionable in its development. To John Wright it seemed (and he grieved because of it) that too many of the "new" liberal Catholics had no tolerance for those who loved ancient things or defended ancient traditions and values. He continued to love and defend them (whether he was right or wrong on any particular issue, theological or disciplinary, is not the question here) and at the same time to reach out to love the world. To the end he was *Sacerdos et Pontifex,* Priest and Bridgebuilder, as we used to sing when a bishop entered a church.

Wright's great hero was John Henry Newman, precisely because Newman combined deep love of and loyalty to the faith with deep love and understanding of the world. For this reason he established an Oratory in his diocese of Pittsburgh in 1961.

He established it "in the spirit of Newman" and set it among the city's secular universities with the hope and the prayer that it might be a community where love of the Church and love of liberal values — learning, freedom, civility, art — might come together. As much as anything else he did, his foundation of the Oratory defined the man; to so love, and serve, the good things of the world that we do not lose those things which are eternal.

More than anyone I've ever known, John Wright had the virtue of piety, *pietas*, in the Virgilian sense. He was not, as far as I know, an admirer of the eighteenth century. In fact, he probably hated it for its rationalism. But Alexander Pope's warning in the "Essay on Man" was part of Wright's natural wisdom: "Be not the first by whom the new is tried / Nor yet the last to lay the old aside." His *pietas* made the cardinal impatient, often furious, with those who had "itching ears." All should be tested and tempered, John Wright thought. One should not easily abandon traditions that have grown from the accumulated experience of history. Like Edmund Burke, he believed that the man who marries the spirit of the age will soon be a widower.

Such views did not always help John Wright's popularity in the post-Vatican II Church. But, I think, they kept him wise and made him great. Lord, grant him eternal rest; and let perpetual light shine upon him. Bishop, Cardinal, Friend; Farewell.

SERMONS

The Feast of the Lord's Baptism

Isaiah 42:1–4, 6–7 / Acts 10:34–38 / Matthew 3:13–17

━ The days of Christmas end today. In our secular culture Christmas ended, I suppose, on New Year's Day. In the mind of the Church, however, and in theological reality today is still Christmas. Today Christmas ends. And the way it ends is, I think, a paradigm of the Christian view of human history and of human life itself. That which begins in humility and in humiliation ends in glory. Today is another manifestation, another epiphany of the power and the mercy of God shown forth to all the nations.

We began the Christmas celebration with a child born in all humility. Without our celebrations last Sunday and today, without the epiphany and the baptism of the Lord (the two go together), the nativity's meaning would be obscured; it would be mere humiliation. It would be the cross without the resurrection. It would be birth and then early death: an obscurity. But the Christian hope and the Christian proclamation is the proclamation that St. Paul makes in the great fifteenth chapter of Corinthians when he speaks of the general resurrection. Paul asks how we are to understand the resurrection of the dead. We must understand it in this way: what begins in corruption ends in incorruption. And those things which are merely mortal take on immortality through Christ. That which is base, in the plan of God, is made golden. And this extends unto all the human race. In the symbolism of the wise men; in the symbolism of Christ's baptism: this child who was born in humility, obscure and unknown and destined according to nature only for death, is proclaimed as the salvation of all the nations. Christ is present everywhere.

Christ is present in the poverty of our spirit and changes it. Christ is present in our moments of despair and rescues us from them. And, yes, Christ is present even in our sin. And that's a bold thing to say. Christ is present in our sin because even in the act of sin, which covers all our lives, in that very act is the invitation to reconciliation and forgiveness. We cannot sin, if we have faith, without knowing that even in the moment of sin we are invited to repentance and to forgiveness. St. John in his first letter said it forever. When we sin, he said, we have an advocate with the Father, Jesus Christ the Righteous. And Christ is the propitiation for our sin. His mercy is at once universally available, and it is present everywhere throughout the world and history.

It is the mission of the Church through history, in whatever culture, in whatever time and place, to proclaim the hope and the ultimate significance of Christ, which is mercy and rescue. "I have come," Christ said, applying the words of the prophet Isaiah (61:1–2) to himself, "I have come to proclaim liberty to the captives and deliverance to those who are in prison, freedom [especially freedom from fear] to all peoples." Christ is everywhere.

Christ is in the most obscure forms. Christ is potentially present in every religion. There is a wonderful book by a Hindu who became a Christian priest. He wrote a book called *The Unknown Christ of Hinduism.* Christ is the fulfillment of all potential, both human and divine. And in the words of one of the greatest of contemporary Roman Catholic theologians, Henri de Lubac, in his book *Catholicism: A Study in the Corporate Destiny of Mankind*, "Christ is the form that humanity must put on, fully to be itself." Because for humanity, in the Christian view, fully to be itself it must realize its glory as well as its humiliation, its immortality as well as its prospect of death. It must look beyond the visible to the invisible. It must know hope. And the name of that hope is Jesus Christ: now proclaimed in the Christmas mystery to all of the nations. And so I say to you again, Merry Christmas, on this last day of Christmas. Rejoice in the Lord.

The Feast of Candlemas

Nehemiah 8:2-4, 5-6, 8-10 / 1 Corinthians 12:12-30 /
Luke 1:1-4; 4:14-21

▬ John bears witness: This is he, the one on whom the Spirit descended. This is the promised and the desired one, not only of Israel but of all the nations. This Jesus is the Son of God.

Here we have the essential faith of the Church: the faith upon which the Church rests, the faith without which the Church would not be the Church, the faith which the Church must protect through the ages against a variety of assaults.

I'd like us to think about this essential faith and relate it to the great second reading in Paul from the first letter to the Corinthians (1 Cor. 12:12-30). In this reading Paul speaks of the rich diversity which should exist within the Church of God. Paul reminds us that within the Church there are a variety of ministries. Some are called to be preachers. Some are called to be teachers. Some are called to be prophets. Within all of this diversity there is a basic unity. Without diversity the Church is stultified. Without unity the Church is destroyed. Within the Church, unity and diversity must coexist in tension. When either is threatened, when either takes dominance, the Church loses its rich character as the Church. It either descends into chaos

Heinz Memorial Chapel, 27 January 1980

and loses the essence of doctrine or it becomes, what Catholicism has appeared to be at certain points in human history, a kind of totalitarian monolith. The danger from either extreme is equal.

Since the Reformation, we Roman Catholics have prided ourselves on our unity. "We believe in one holy, Catholic and apostolic Church." Few in the Church today, however, would disagree that from the Council of Trent up through the Second Vatican Council the unity we prided ourselves on was a defense against what we saw as the chaos and sectarianism of our Protestant brethren. (Actually, we didn't see them as brethren in those days. We saw them as enemies.) Nonetheless, we prided ourselves on our unity; to be a Catholic was to agree on everything. Given conditions such as these, the rich diversity of the Church was in danger of being lost.

On the other hand, the unity of the Church since Vatican II has in some instances been threatened by diversity. All diversity in the Church must be measured against the rock of the Church's faith: the faith proclaimed, upheld, fought over, argued, and in many cases died for over the centuries; the faith proclaimed by John the Baptist: This is the Son of God on whom God's favor rests. This is the salvation of the nations. This Jesus is no mere creature. He is the Eternal Word. In him shines forth the glory of God. Any diversity within the Church which in the name of freedom threatens this essence of the Catholic faith is not Catholic and it is the Church's duty to say it is not Catholic. This is not to deny freedom. It is to protect what is essential. That is the Church's duty.

There is much controversy now and many are pained and I myself am pained by certain procedures which continue to exist within the Church. But it is the procedures I would protest against in the theological investigations against [Hans] Küng and [Edward] Schillebeeckx. I would not, however, protest the Church's duty to protect the faith. This is the faith of the Church: "Thou art the Christ, the Son of the living God" (John 6:69). "This is my beloved Son on whom my favor rests. Hear him" (Mark 1:11). Throughout the ages, it is the duty of the Church to protect this teaching.

The Third Sunday in Ordinary Time

Isaiah 8:23–9, 3 / 1 Corinthians 1:10–13, 17 / Matthew 4:12–23

■ In the first reading from the prophet Isaiah and repeated at the beginning of the Gospel according to Matthew, the mighty promise of the Church and of all who believe in Christ is recalled to us. "The people who walked in darkness have seen a great light. And on those who sit in the shadow of death a mighty light has dawned" (Isa. 9:1–2). We are recalled to that light and to its meaning: especially on this Sunday, the feast of the Conversion of St. Paul the Apostle. On this Sunday the churches which profess the name of Christ pray that those who believe in Christ may not obscure the light who is Christ nor dampen that hope which he is. At the same time we confess that we who believe in Christ have osbcured the light, have dampened the hope.

Where we who profess Christ should have proclaimed light, we have frequently extinguished light and left the nations in darkness. And we who should have been reconcilers have been dividers, and we who should have been sowers of hope have often created dispair. For all these things the churches, especially on this day, and we ourselves individually are called to repentance. We are called to self-criticism. We are called to the effort, both psychological and historical, of breaking down those

Heinz Memorial Chapel, 25 January 1981

things which we have set up to divide us, the effort as well of seeking those things which should unite us.

It's interesting to listen to the words of St. Paul in the very earliest days of the Church when he wrote to the Corinthians: "Has Christ been divided?" he asked (1 Cor. 1:13). Are there parties and differences amongst you? Do you distrust and hate each other? Is Christ divided? Christ cannot be divided. Yet we can obscure his unity and we have.

We are divided. We are divided within ourselves. Each of us is split. Each of us is in some way schizophrenic. We are sowers of dissention. The light of Christ is obscured and the nations continue to walk in darkness.

And to what can we recall ourselves when we pray for the unity of the Church? This prayer should not be an exercise in sentimentality. Nor in some form of unreality. It should not be a summons to sacrifice whatever is essential in our faith. But it should be a call to consider what is essential and to consider also what we have labeled essential which is not so. It is a call to psychological and historical realism.

There stands an ancient saying, echoed down the Christian centuries from one of the Church fathers; he gave a guide for all Christians in these matters. "In essential things: unity. In nonessential things: diversity. In all things: charity." At the risk of historical oversimplification (but I think with some truth), it seems to me that especially since the Reformation the Catholic churches (and especially the Roman part of the Catholic Church) have tended to multiply what is essential beyond necessity. Remember, some of you who studied philosophy, Ockham's Razor: do not multiply being without necessity. It's a necessary philosophical axiom and it's also a very necessary theological axiom. Do not multiply being without necessity. Do not multiply the essentials of faith without necessity.

There can be no doubt that the Roman Catholic Church since

the Council of Trent has tended to multiply the necessities of faith beyond necessity. Look back at your own youth and all those things which seemed so necessary to being a Catholic, so necessary to the unity of the Church. They are now subjects for caricature. The mass everywhere had to be in Latin. There was a suppression of dissent, theological and philosophical, within the Church. The Church, largely from the sixteenth century on, took as its model an army and as its motto a strict discipline. All these things were multiplying what it is to be Catholic, without necessity.

To be Catholic is to preach the universality of Jesus Christ. To recall the words of Henri de Lubac: "Christ is the form that humanity must put on, truly to be itself." But if we can say this about ourselves (and I think that we should, those of us who are Roman Catholic; I presume most of us here are, although we're not quite so sure what that means as we were twenty years ago and what is essential to it), then I think we can say that our brothers in Christ from the Reformation tradition have perhaps in many instances erred in the second part: they have made more things nonessential that are essential. And the unity of the Church has to be achieved by bringing these two together and in harmony.

I can't remember whether I heard him say it or I read it, but Paul Tillich said that the unity of the Church can only be achieved, the new Catholic Church will only emerge, from a reunion of Catholic substance with Protestant protest. The two have to come together. We must have Catholic substance, not multiplied, but those things which are essential to the faith: the transcendence of God touching man in Christ Jesus and the universality of his salvation. And our unity in the sacraments, in the eucharist, in the historic Church. But within unity there must be much diversity. There must be much Protestant protest. We must have a Catholic Church in which the Protestant principle is operative. Or it will not be the true Church of Jesus Christ. It will be an army rather than Christ's mystical body. To this end, an effort at psychological and historical criticism, at corporate and individual examination is required. It is a painful process to work toward a truly Catholic Church. It will not take place in a generation. But thank God it's begun to take place.

In my own boyhood such an effort would have been of no concern to the Catholics of my generation; we had the Truth. As I think about it, we talked about Protestantism as though it were another faith. The Catholic faith and the Protestant faith! "Is Christ divided?" There is not a Protestant baptism as opposed to a Catholic baptism. There is one baptism: "In the name of the Father and of the Son and of the Holy Spirit."

We are all new people in Christ. Let us pray and work and study and think that we may find the proper way to be truly and fully a new people in Christ: tolerating diversity but holding fast to what is essential, those really few things that we profess in the creed that are essential. And so to show forth the light of Christ to the nations and his hope to all the peoples who still walk in darkness two millennia after Christ and who still sit in the shadow of death.

The Fourth Sunday in Ordinary Time

Zephaniah 2:3; 3:12–13 / 1 Corinthians 1:26–31 / Matthew 5:1–12

━━ I can not recollect any other Sunday scriptures that bring us so close to the heart of the gospel and lead us so far away from the wisdom of this world. These readings are an affront to worldly wisdom. They are a rock to shatter our complacency. They are foolishness according to everything the world values. They are a challenge cast at bourgeois society and middle-class values. They are foolishness; they are folly according to all the standards on which contemporary or any modern civilization rests. They speak of defeat as being victory. They speak of mourning as being something to be hoped for. They speak of poverty, rejection, and persecution as things to be desired be- cause through them we come to God's kingdom. In a word, these scriptures speak of the things God chooses. St. Paul says, "It was to shame the wise that he chose what is foolish by human reckoning and to shame what is strong that he chose what is weak by human reckoning" (1 Cor. 1:28).

In Matthew's version of the Beatitudes we read: "Blessed are those who mourn; they shall be comforted" (Matt. 5:5). In Luke's more poignant version we read: "Blessed are you who weep now; you shall laugh" (Luke 6:21). Without weeping there is no final laughter. Without denuding ourselves of our material and our

Heinz Memorial Chapel, 1 February 1981

psychological illusions, there is no coming to ultimate reality. The Beatitudes are so central to the meaning of the gospel that in the liturgy of the Eastern churches they are part of every liturgy. At every mass in the Western church the Lord's Prayer is said; at every liturgy in the Orthodox church the Beatitudes are sung together by the choir and all the people. These blessings take us to the heart of what Christianity is all about. Furthermore, they remind us of some essential truths about ourselves.

We are all beggars before God. We are all weak. We are all poor. We are all foolish. Our strength, our riches, or whatever wisdom we might have — all come, finally, not from ourselves nor from the philosophy of this world nor from the values of this or any other civilization, but come rather from God himself. "The foolish things of this world has God chosen in order to confound the wise." In the words of the great song of the Blessed Virgin Mary, the Magnificat: "He fills the hungry with good things and the rich he sends away empty. He casts down the mighty from their thrones and he raises up the lowly and the meek" (Luke 1:52–53). God loves those who are in greatest need.

God loves us in our weakness. Indeed, if one can speak of God's despising anything (and to speak of God at all is to speak by analogy), then using human language, we can say God despises those who think themselves strong. God despises those who rule. God despises those who savor power. God forgets those who are full of worldly things. "Beware, you who are filled now; you shall be empty. Beware, you who laugh now, you shall weep" (Luke 6:25). These things are the very heart of the gospel. We are all beggars before God, the Beatitudes remind us. We are all fools before God. We are all weak and we are all foolish. After all, wisdom in any human terms is at best a very poor and quite relative thing. Human wisdom is a mere approximation of what wisdom truly is. Wisdom is God.

The Beatitudes call us to this remembrance. Those of us who think we are wise are reminded how foolish we are. Those of us who think we are rich are reminded how poor we are. Those of us who think we are strong are reminded how weak we are. It is only those who know their need for God and who know that their fulfillment is not in themselves but only in God: it is only those who shall be full; it is only those who shall rejoice; it is only those who will not suffer a final disappointment.

The day will come when we shall lose all that we value. Where are our riches? They will pass away. Whom do we love? We shall lose them. What awaits us? The grave. All else shall be gone. God alone shall remain. He is our beginning; he is our end.

To ponder these things as they are set forth in the Beatitudes is to come to the very heart of Christianity.

The Fifth Sunday in Ordinary Time

Isaiah 58:7-10 / 1 Corinthians 2:1-5 / Matthew 5:13-16

■ The words that St. Paul wrote to the Corinthians in the earliest days of the Church have been assigned as a witness and as a mark of the Church throughout the ages. "The only knowledge I claimed to have was about Jesus, and only about him as the crucified Christ" (1 Cor. 2:2).

It is the mission of the Church to preach Jesus Christ crucified and risen. The Church must so preach among all the nations. The Church must so preach until the end of time. If the Church does not preach this, if the Church abandons the preaching of the mystery of the cross and the resurrection in pursuit of any temporal good, no matter how necessary or how laudable that temporal good may be, the Church not only forsakes its mission but the Church becomes irrelevant to the ultimate human condition. Because the ultimate human condition lies beyond time. Because the ultimate human condition ends in eternity. And it is the claim of the Church that this ultimate destiny is made possible by Christ dying and rising again.

There has been great confusion in the Church, especially since Vatican II, about what it is relevant for the Church to do. I've heard over the years various comments, various people (including friends) saying that our preaching is not relevant: "You're

Heinz Memorial Chapel, 8 February 1981

not talking about the social issues of the day. What about the problem of discrimination? What about economic problems?" If you want that kind of preaching, go to the Unitarian church. What could be more relevant than our destiny? What could be deeper than our souls? That is what the Church preaches. The Church addresses itself to what is ultimate: to what we are in our deepest beings—heirs to a kingdom. And, of course, the Church must be the servant of the poor. The prophet Isaiah reminds us of that in the first lesson we heard: "Thus says the Lord, 'Share your bread with the hungry and bring the homeless poor into your own house. And when you see those who are naked, cover them. And then shall your light rise in darkness and cause light throughout the whole world'" (58:7-8).

This service to which we are also called must be put, though, in its priority. And it is a consequence—a consequence of the first thing which the Church preaches, which is Jesus Christ. Jesus Christ is the first word which the Church addresses to us and insists upon. Jesus Christ is our ultimate destiny. The sacrament of the eucharist is the sign of the eternal banquet which is our destiny, a destiny made possible through the unique act of God in giving himself in his Eternal Word, his Son, for our salvation. If the Church forgets to preach this, then the Church is damned, the Church is lost. The Church then makes itself merely another agency for political or social change. I reiterate: we must be concerned with these things, but as a consequence of the love of Jesus Christ poured forth upon us and our consequent vocation to show this mercy and this light in our own lives and in our own acts.

The Church preaches something which Paul understood so profoundly and preached so insistently. Paul is so wise. Paul is the greatest genius I can think of in Christian history. Everything is in St. Paul. His priorities are right. He knows the centrality of the cross. He knows the final promise of the resurrection. In another place Paul says, "If I preach anything but Jesus Christ and him crucified and risen, let me be damned; I have forsaken my vocation." What would happen if the best social engineering, the best technology, the most equitable economic system we can devise came into being and we then discovered there was nothing in us beyond that? I remember years ago reading a wonderful article by a Swedish correspondent for *Commonweal* magazine. The article was called "Why the Swedes Are Sad." Sweden at that time had and maybe still has the most advanced social welfare system of any nation in the world. This author/correspondent explained that the Swedes are sad because the whole sense of religion has been lost in the pursuit of technology, in the pursuit of human wisdom.

There is a void and a darkness and a despair in the heart of these people, in our hearts too, if we forget that man does not live by bread alone. Man lives by the word that comes out of the mouth of God, spoken by Jesus Christ. This is our ultimate strength; this is our ultimate hope. But it is not, as St. Paul says here, the wisdom of this world. Because the wisdom of this world could never guess at such things. The wisdom of this world and its philosophies would never discover the cross and could never come to faith in the resurrection.

Technology, science, philosophy, economics: they speak to us of necessary things that pass. And if that's all there is, we are left with despair. The Church and the gospel rescue us from despair. They speak to us of things too profound to be uttered in any merely human language. The Church speaks to us of the deep things of God. And in so doing it speaks to us of the deepest things in ourselves. In the words of St. Augustine, "Our hearts were made for you, O God, and they are restless until they find their rest in you."

This is the ultimate wisdom. This is the gift of God which we here celebrate and preach.

The Seventh Sunday in Ordinary Time

Leviticus 19:1-2, 17-18 / 1 Corinthians 3:16-23 / Matthew 5:38-48

■ St. Paul tells us, as he told the Corinthians to whom he was writing: "God's foolishness is wiser than human wisdom and God's weakness is stronger than human strength" (1 Cor. 1:25). The wisdom of God is folly to this world. If you wish to become wise, then you must become a fool for the sake of Christ.

St. Paul here gives the lie to all forms of bourgeois religion, to all forms of religion which reduce religion to good conduct, which reduce religion to some ethical code. One does not need religion in order to become just. In order to become holy, however, one does need God; one does need religion. Holiness and justice are quite different. Holiness utterly transcends the concept of ethics or of justice.

The gospel words of Christ are surely, according to any standards of this world, an ultimate example of foolishness. I daresay that few of us could even remotely think of taking them seriously. "Love your enemies; do good to those who hate you; bless those who curse you; pray for those who treat you badly" (Luke 6:27-28). This is utter foolishness according to all of the standards of this world. It stands in contradiction to all conventional and middle-class wisdom.

Heinz Memorial Chapel, 22 February 1981

Foolishness! That is what we are called to. That is what Paul is here talking about. Paul insists that what he is preaching is mere foolishness to this world: the folly of the cross (and what could be more foolish than the cross?). Here for all to see is the foolishness of God's Eternal Word, mocked and spat upon and bearing it all without complaint, fulfilling thereby in himself the words of the prophet Isaiah: "He turned not his face from shame and spitting" (50:6). He uttered no complaint. More, he loved and forgave those who spat upon him, those who rebuffed him and subjected him to ultimate contempt, those who nailed him to that ultimate foolishness which is the cross and all that the cross stands for.

We are called, not to the wisdom of this world, but rather to holiness, a concept which belongs to God alone. In the Gloria that we say every Sunday and every major feast day, we affirm of God: "You alone are holy." And it is to holiness, the holiness of God, that today's scriptures call us. In the reading from Leviticus we are told: "You must be holy because I, the Lord your God, am holy" (Lev. 19:1). Holiness is a concept utterly beyond human wisdom. Holiness, in fact, is the foolishness of God. St. Paul tells us, again in Corinthians and in conjunction with what he is telling us about the foolishness of God, that "the Holy Spirit dwells in you and therefore you must be holy because God's temple is holy and you are that temple." As God's temple, you have been snatched out by grace from what is merely human, from your merely human condition with all its finitude. You are God-bearers.

Right now, at this moment in history, you are walking around bearing God. Such a way of thinking about yourself must always remain foolishness to this world. At the same time it makes terrible demands upon you. You are God's temple. You are holy because of the Holy Spirit's activity working within you. These, when they are thought on and deeply felt, are shattering concepts. They are concepts that carry with them a certain grandeur because holiness — again, I say, not good conduct — holiness is grandeur and majesty, of a kind and degree pertaining to God alone. As Christians, because of God's generosity, we share in the grandeur and majesty of God's holiness.

But what makes us holy? We are a holy people because we have been seized by God and set apart by him to be sharers in his own divine and holy life.

I happened this morning to read a book review in the *Times Literary Supplement* [13 February 1981] which, strangely enough on this day when the readings are about the foolishness of Christ, commented on a new release from Oxford University Press called *Perfect Fools.* The book itself quotes one of the greatest — some consider him in fact the greatest — of contemporary Roman Catholic theologians, the Swiss thinker Hans Urs von Balthazar. The reviewer, Anthony Burgess, quotes von Balthazar: "We have to be transported by the very concept of God." The experience of faith, the experience of God in the life of faith, is a matter of rhapsody and glory. It cannot be contained in any logic or in any syllogism or in any system of philosophy, or, to use St. Paul's terms — in any "wisdom of this world." This word is folly; it cannot be contained in a syllogism nor can it be reduced to what is merely proper and ethical. Proper and ethical conduct is, of course, a good thing; it belongs, however, to the order of nature. The concept of holiness, on the other hand, and the foolishness of God belong to the order of that grace by which we are touched, by which we are seized.

Again in this review, Burgess quotes St. Bernard of Clairvaux: Faith is a kind of "sober inebriation," a kind of drunkenness. It seizes us and takes us out of ourselves, out of our fallen and finite egos. It transports us into a realm of undreamed of glory which is the Realm of God, the Realm we show forth in the liturgy, the Realm to which the sacraments and the Church are the bridge by which we pass over from the ordinary to the utterly extraordinary, from nature to grace, from finitude to infinity, from ethics to holiness.

Thinking on these things, we realize that Christ is the ultimate fool, just as his words to us in the gospel seem ultimate folly. His words give the lie to this world. We Christians, however, do not belong only to this world. We move through it. We try to serve it. We try to better it. And we are called to love it. But we are not prisoners of it.

Already we belong to another world, the world whose fulfillment is God. And that's our life. As St. Paul again says today: We belong not to Paul nor to Apollo. No! We belong only to Christ. In him all past and all future is contained. Because of this, because we belong only to Christ, all things are ours. "Everything is yours because you are Christ's and Christ is God's."

The First Sunday of Lent

Deuteronomy 26:4–10 / Romans 10:8–13 / Luke 4:1–13

■ The time is fulfilled. The kingdom of God is at hand. Repent and believe the gospel. Turn away from your false idols and come once again to the living and only God. Dare to believe that this God heals you, that you are not locked into the way you are, that you can become things you had not dreamed of. Dare to believe that you are touched by God's glory, that you are heir to his promise.

This is the good news of Lent. This is the mighty promise that sustains us and renews us during these sacred forty days as the Church prepares for our greatest celebration: the Lord's resurrection.

Before the liturgy began, Gregory Lehane, a friend of mine and our master of ceremonies, said that Americans like Lent. We get, it's true, huge crowds here on Ash Wednesday. And Gregory said Americans like Lent because it appeals to the deep puritanism in the American character and to the puritanism that especially marks Irish-American Catholicism. More people come to the liturgy on Ash Wednesday than come on holy days of obligation. Everyone loves to receive ashes and to walk around and show them to everyone else even though the gospel says, "When you fast, wash your face." Probably because it was deeply

Heinz Memorial Chapel, 24 February 1980

ingrained during our childhood, many of us retain a notion of
Lent that is not only deeply puritanical but deeply formalistic
and legalistic. Lent was a time for not doing things that we liked
to do. Because it was a gloomy time, it appealed to a deep puritanism in all of us.

But gloominess is the opposite of what Lent is all about. Lent
is a time of profound hope. Lent is a time of profound renewal.
Lent, properly understood, is psychologically and theologically
a profoundly joyous time.

The first reading we heard today speaks of deliverance, of
the mighty acts of God in delivering his people Israel through
the Red Sea from slavery into freedom. Each Lent we are reminded of our freedom, which is Jesus Christ, and of our deliverance, which is his resurrection. We are reminded that we
must not remain as we are. We are further reminded that the
possibility of change is ever open to us. One of the despairs that
many people know (and I think it is a common despair of middle
age, a fact often remarked upon by psychologists) is that we
feel trapped in ourselves. We feel trapped in what we are. Some
feel trapped in a marriage which isn't very happy. Some feel
trapped in a location which doesn't bring fulfilment. Some feel
trapped in tight and worrisome economic circumstances. Most
feel trapped (perhaps a better word is cheated or disappointed)
when the realization comes sometime in life that not all of one's
dreams are going to be fulfilled; indeed, that many of one's young
dreams are going to be disappointed.

During this season, however, the Church comes to tell us:
You are not trapped. This Egypt of your present life is not your
eternal condition. The path to freedom and to change is constantly offered to you in Jesus Christ. Return to me, says the
Lord, and you shall receive my light. Return to me and cast aside
your false gods and you too will make the recurring journey

from despair and disappointment into new expectation and new hope.

You can change. And as often as you have changed to what you would want you can recover the vision. Though you relapse and lose the vision, you can regain the former clarity of sight. And the vision and the faith and the hope and the love can come back to you. Cardinal Newman said: "To live is to change and to live deeply is to change often."

The church invites us to change. Her invitation is not puritanical. Her invitation is not gloomy. This is joyous hope: the joyous hope that we prepare for in these days of awaiting the resurrection.

Lent also reminds us of another profound thing — something I like to return to again and again in thinking about the gospel. Every time we come together as a worshiping community, every time we make the profession of faith in the creed, we affirm the intersection of the sacred and the secular. We affirm that we who are believing people live in two orders. We live in the order of that which is trivial. We live in the order of mortality. We live in the order, being mortal, that is overshadowed by death. We are those people of whom Isaiah speaks, "people who live in the land of deep shadow" (9:2). But we are also another kind of people, and this is much more important for us. We are a people who live in another order which overcomes the first order; we live in the order of God, the sacred order, and in a sacred time, a special time such as Lent. We are made aware that the sacred order has intersected our purely secular order and has cut our utter dependence upon it. Already, God's promise is working amongst us. The kingdom of God is at hand and you live in its joyful promise.

These might be the things that we think on during Lent — the casting out of the idols of triviality from our lives, the turning again away from our idols to the only true God, the repentance of our slavery to the things that are trivial, the renewal of our ultimate allegiance to those things which shall last forever; to take both God and ourselves with the utmost seriousness once again, to do those things which will renew us, not through any formalism or externality or puritanism but rather by taking ourselves and our God seriously. Thus we shall prepare ourselves for the glory of the resurrection. Thus we shall be certain of sharing in Christ's radiance.

The Third Sunday of Lent

Exodus 17:3–7 / Romans 5:1–2, 5–8 / John 4:5–42

━━ In the fourth chapter of the Gospel of St. John we read the story of Christ and the Samaritan woman, a stranger. We read of his promise to her of a living water, a new kind of life that would spring up through faith for all who believed in him. We read of her acceptance of this promise, her acceptance of Jesus as the Christ, the source of new life and of a living water. Surely this is one of the most beautiful chapters in St. John. And it deserves endless pondering.

The Samaritan woman's spiritual saga is closely related to Paul's wisdom about our justification through faith: the new life of peace and of reconciliation that comes to us through this justification. Here is a life and here is a hope that will not disappoint us because, as Paul so wonderfully says "Now that we have been justified by faith, we are at peace with God through our Lord Jesus Christ" (Rom. 5:1).

We can be at peace, even in the face of separation and death. We can be at peace because hope does not disappoint us and God's own hope, God's own love, have been poured into our hearts by the gift of the Holy Spirit, through Christ Jesus received in faith. This is the gospel. This is the good news. We are reconciled. Grace, the living water, has overcome our aliena-

Heinz Memorial Chapel, 22 March 1981

tion and our ultimate sadness and our despair: the very stuff of which a life without faith is constructed. There is no way to escape it without faith. But, thanks be to God, we are not finally separated; we are not finally alienated; we are not finally dead. We live! Because those who, in Christ Jesus, partake of this living water, this grace, this reconciliation, have a spring within them, through hope, a well which springs up unto eternal life. Those who drink of this refreshment will not die forever. The victory has been achieved. Separation is overcome. Sin is conquered. Life is given unto us. The thirst that in the deepest recesses of every human spirit is felt, along with the hunger for the ultimate, is filled. Those who drink of Jesus Christ will not thirst forever. Those who hunger after God shall be filled. Our hope will not be disappointed because the grace of God has been poured forth in our hearts by the Holy Spirit and we are at peace and we are consoled.

If we meditate upon this, if we grasp this profound meaning for our lives and for our hope, then we can be at peace in the face of the worst sorrow and the worst disappointment, all separation and adversity. We are an alienated people. We are a separated people. And this is what the doctrine of original sin means. We are born in separation. In his sermon titled "You Are Accepted," Paul Tillich rightly defines sin as "separation." Sin separates us from each other. Sin separates us from ourselves. As the apostle said, "I recognize a war is going on within me. I do those things which I ought not to do." I do those things that I do not want to do and I leave undone those things which I ought to do and want to do. And he said: "How shall I be delivered from the body of this death?" — this kind of alienation and separation. And then he immediately cries out: "Thanks be to God through Jesus Christ" (Rom. 7:24). I have been delivered through the grace of our Lord Jesus Christ, the living water. I have been delivered because God's grace is stronger than our sin and his reconciling power is greater than our separation. And that's why Paul cries out in another place: "Where sin abounds, grace abounds even more."

Our weakness can not stand up against God's strength. And our separation can not stand up against God's reconciling power in Jesus Christ. And the separations in our lives are brought together by God's healing power. We are a "healed" people because grace abounds in our life. Grace is acceptance. We are accepted. As Paul says today: "While we were yet sinners, Christ died for us" (Rom. 5:8). And God accepts us. And God heals our wounds. And God draws us to himself. And God gives us hope. And hope gives us peace. And so, for all these things, we say: "Thanks be to God."

The Fifth Sunday of Lent

Ezekiel 37:12–14 / Romans 8:8–11 / John 11:1–45

━━ This used to be called Passion Sunday. Still it is the Sunday on which the Church begins the season of Passiontide, her immediate preparation for the mysteries of the passion, death, and resurrection of the Lord. No scripture could be more appropriate than today's account from St. John's gospel of Lazarus and his resurrection through the power of Jesus. We, all of us together as believing Christians and some of us who perhaps struggle to believe, are about to enter into the most profound thing the Christian Church has to offer.

The cry is heard, "God desires life, not death." We learn for the first time or again why Jesus came to the day and hour of his suffering. We learn that he did not come as some social reformer, not as some political figure; these things are revealed in all their triviality by comparison to what he came as. He came as life itself. He came as the triumph over death, as the light which casts out all darkness.

These are the deep mysteries of the gospel. This is the triumphant claim that Christianity makes. This is the mystery to which the Church invites us, with great urgency and love and profundity, to enter into. What begins today continues through Good Friday, until during the Easter vigil we make our mighty

Heinz Memorial Chapel, 5 April 1981

affirmation and sing the Exultet; we proclaim that death is conquered in Christ.

But first of all we are all Lazarus. Before we can triumph, we must suffer and die. Victory is not easy and grace is not cheap. They are dearly bought with hard struggle; they do not exist through denial of the hard reality of life and of the grave. "Unless the seed fall into the ground and die, it cannot live." Christianity is not some form of the denial of the hardness and the bitterness and the disappointment of human life. And I can think of no passage in the gospels that I personally find more moving than the grief of Jesus: "Jesus wept" (John 11:36). He was not a magician. "Jesus groaned inwardly in his spirit" (John 11:38). He was not saying resurrection is easy or that coming to the light is an easy thing or that the victory over death is an easy thing. He keeps insisting (in the readings that the Church gives us in these days) that before the Son of Man can be raised up he must first suffer and know all manner of rejection and die. Only then will victory be attained. The reality of death and separation is not evaded in this story of Lazarus. The reality of death and separation is faced starkly and the truth of our own situation is set baldly before us. Before we exalt with Christ, we first must weep with him and suffer with him and groan inwardly in our spirit with him, even as he wept, suffered, and inwardly groaned over the death of Lazarus whom he loved.

As we shall be repeatedly reminded during these coming days of Passiontide, the mystery of Christ means that in Christ, the Eternal Word, God has entered most profoundly into the worst suffering and deprivation that we can feel in our own spirit and in our own life. Do we weep? God wept. Do we suffer? God suffered. Do we die? In Christ, God died. Do we live? Yes! Because God raised Jesus from the dead and raises us up with him.

God's design for us, revealed in Christ, is that our end is life not death. And this is the profundity of the Lazarus story in all its realism and with all its pathos and in all its moving drama.

St. Paul says to the Romans in the second reading: "If you are only in the flesh, you die." Because the flesh by itself cannot live. The flesh, by definition, is that which dies. But we are not one dimensional. To be without faith is to lead a one-dimensional existence; and a one-dimensional existence ends only in death. But faith raises us up from a one-dimensional existence. It raises us up to the kingdom of God, of which we are already members through baptism and through faith. The Church now asks us to stir up our faith and our hope, to face the reality of our fate in the fate of Jesus, prefigured in the fate of Lazarus, but to look beyond our fate to what God promises in the life, in the mystery, and in the victory of Jesus Christ.

Holy Thursday

Exodus 12:1–8, 11–14 / 1 Corinthians 11:23–26 / John 13:1–15

■ This is the Passover of the Lord. This solemn day is the beginning of our Passover. In the sacred mysteries of the passion and the death of the Lord, by which we come to the glory of the resurrection and by which alone we come to the glory of the resurrection, we, in a much more marvelous way than our ancestors, the people of Israel, make a mighty Passover. The people of Israel passed through the waters of the Red Sea, led by the Lord from slavery to freedom. And so in these days do we pass through Jesus Christ. But the slavery and the freedom that are ours are more profound than the slavery and the freedom that were the lot of the children of Israel. We are touched and altered not by any external condition of our lives nor by the geography of our habitation, but touched rather by the most profound psychological and spiritual slavery and freedom. It is from fear to hope that we pass over, from darkness to light.

This is the Passover of the Lord and it is our own Passover. What Jesus did this day — which we commemorate with great solemnity, with sorrow, but also with hope and joy — what Jesus did this day gives us the key to his and our Passover.

This day is called Maundy Thursday. "Maundy," the Old English word for this day, means it is the Thursday of the Com-

Heinz Memorial Chapel, 16 April 1981

mandment; "maundy" is the Old English corruption of the Latin *mandatum:* the "commandment." This is the day on which we observe and remember the two great and related commandments of the Lord. The basic commandment is the commandment of love. "This commandment I give unto you: that you love one another in the way," and here is the operative clause, *"in the way* that I have loved you" (John 15:12). Jesus does not merely command us to love one another. More intensely and more specifically he commands us: "Love one another *in the way* that I have loved you." And the way in which Christ loved us, of course, is symbolized in what he did at the Last Supper: the utter humiliation of washing his friends' feet.

St. Paul reveals the meaning of this great symbol in the lyrical language of his immortal poem: "Christ, though he was in the form of God, did not consider his Godhead a thing to be coveted, but rather he emptied himself and he took the form of a servant. And for this reason the Father has glorified him and has given him a name that is above every other name, so that at the name of Jesus every knee should bend, of those that are on this earth and those that are in heaven itself" (Phil. 2:6–11). He emptied himself and therefore he was glorified. Self-emptying love is the first and most basic of the Christian commandments, because, as St. Paul tells us: "If I have all the eloquence of men and of angels, but speak without love, I am simply a gong booming and a cymbal clashing" (1 Cor. 13:1).

The love we are commanded to practice, the love with which Christ has loved us, is a self-emptying love. It is a love that seeks not self, but seeks a passage out of the prison of one's self, of one's own egoism, and a passage into service. A few of us achieve this, but it is a lofty thing to which we and the whole Church are called: to be a servant of a reconciling and a loving Church, a humble Church, a questioning Church, a pilgrim

Church seeking to serve, seeking to pursue that thing we call "God" through the Church's mysteries and signs.

The eucharist, of course, is related to this pursuit. Part, and perhaps the most profound part of the self-emptying of Christ, was the sharing of his divine life with us in the sacrament of his body and his blood. "I will not leave you orphans" (John 14:18). "Know that I am with you always; yes, to the end of time" (Matt. 28:20). And the kingdom of God is among us each time we fulfill the other part of the commandment: "Do this in memory of me" (Luke 22:19). Because, as St. Paul tells us, each time we come together "to eat this bread and drink this cup" (1 Cor. 11:27), we show forth the death of the Lord and what he has done for us in his self-emptying until he comes again. He is with us sacramentally as a sign of ultimate self-giving.

"God is love," as St. John tells us, "and anyone who lives in love lives in God and God lives in him." But love is not easy. The love of Christ and the love of God in Christ was not easy. It was a terrible love, a terrible thing, this self-emptying. It called forth the groaning in the garden: "Father, if it be possible, let this cup pass from me" (Luke 22:42). In his humanity it seems obvious that Jesus did not completely understand — and certainly in his humanity found it difficult and painful to accept — the demands of self-emptying love. But he followed them: "Not my will but thy will be done" (Luke 22:43). And the gift of the eucharist is the great sign of the ultimate gift of God's life to us. We are not orphans. God is with us. We are not left alone.

One can think of many passages in scripture that, no matter how often one hears them, always deeply stir and grip one. I suppose we all have our own favorites. But, if I lived a thousand years and every Maundy Thursday heard the account of the foot-washing and the response of Peter, I would always be deeply moved, even to tears. Poor Peter who did not fully understand what he was about. Poor Peter with his frequent falls and his denials and his denseness (we can almost call it) in understanding what the Lord was doing. And in this way Peter, perhaps more than any of the other apostles, can speak to us. And perhaps because of his very humanity, Peter became the first of the apostles; because, as St. Paul says, "It is in our weakness that God shows forth his strength," as he did in Peter. And remember poor Peter saying in another place, "Even if I have to die with you, I will never disown you" (Mark 14:31). And, of course, he denied the Lord three times that very night: as we do, all our days. And poor, proud Peter who said, "You shall never wash my feet" (John 13:8). And the Lord said, "Unless I wash your feet, you can have nothing in common with me." And that wonderful response of Peter's: "Then, Lord, not only my feet, but my hands and my head as well" (John 13:9). And that can be our prayer this day: Lord, not only my feet, but my head and my hands and my heart. And make all these things new. And make it possible for me, in all my weakness and silliness, at least at times in my life to fulfill your command of love: to love as you have loved us.

Easter Vigil

Romans 6:3–11 / Mark 16:1–8

━ "'My thoughts are not your thoughts nor are your words my words,' says the Lord. 'For, as the heavens are high above the earth, so are my thoughts and my words high beyond your thoughts and your words'" (Isa. 55:8).

We make tonight a bolder affirmation than the affirmation many of us made here less than four months ago. Less than four months ago many of us came together joyfully to celebrate the mysterious union of God and Man in Jesus, Son of the Eternal Father, born of the Virgin Mary. And, speaking from this pulpit, I tried to remind myself and all of my friends here that what we were celebrating, this beginning of the mystery of our redemption, was not a sentimental thing: it was and it remains a hard thing.

This child whose birth we celebrated was destined for loneliness, for rejection, and for death. He was destined to know everything that we in our worst and most lonely moments could learn. For him was destined the desertion of his friends. For him was destined the bloody sweat. "He turned not his face from shame and spitting" (Isa. 50:6). He knew humiliation. And, yes, on the cross (in the words which we heard again this week), he knew the absence of God. This is a paradox we could think

Heinz Memorial Chapel, 14 April 1979

about each day of our lives — this ultimate paradox, this ultimate mystery — God knew the absence of God.

We have recalled many times that the experience of our age seems to be the experience of God's absence. God seems far away; God perhaps seems farther away than was true for our forefathers. Many now find it impossible to have hope. Many find it impossible to believe in God. Men live in emptiness and in despair. Men give themselves over to gods who not only are less than God but are less than human: the gods of economies, the gods of political ideologies, the gods of psychologism, the gods of sociology — gods who, in a word, all have a speedy ending and die a quick death.

But the God we proclaim here tonight is the God who triumphs over history, a God who undid the work that nature had done to itself. And the theme I set down when I thought about it tonight — the theme I would like to make the subject of our meditation is this: what nature to itself undid, God through the grace of Christ has redone. What nature did to destroy itself, bringing sin and death and despair and emptiness and loneliness (that is, the abolition of the Ultimate), God, by the grace of Christ, by his entering completely into this condition of ours, by his passion, by his death, and by his resurrection has repaired. What nature to itself undid, God in Christ has redone.

I was reading a book recently published — and it's certainly one of the most remarkable books I've ever read — the collected letters of Flannery O'Connor, *The Habit of Being*. She wrote remarkable letters and she died ten years ago at age thirty-nine.

In one of her letters to someone who was having difficulties believing, O'Connor wrote: "To see Christ as God and man is probably no more difficult today than it has always been." It is always a difficult thing. Faith is a hard thing. Faith is not easy.

In another place, Flannery O'Connor says that we tend to see faith — to treat it — as a kind of electric blanket, shielding us and warming us in the night. It is not that. Faith is a cross. Faith demands works. Faith demands response. Faith demands courage. And faith frequently demands what this world regards as mere foolishness.

"My thoughts are not your thoughts," says God, "nor are my ways your ways" (Isa. 55:8). But, Flannery O'Connor goes on in this letter, for many of us today lack of faith is "a matter of not being able to accept a suspension of the laws of the flesh and the physical. For my part, I think that when I know what the laws of the flesh are, then I will know what God is. For me it is the virgin birth, the Incarnation, and the resurrection which are the true laws of the flesh." Death, dissolution, decay, destruction, division: these are all distortions of the flesh and of the physical as God meant them to be in his original creation.

O'Connor continues, "I am always astonished at the emphasis the Church puts on the body." It is not the soul, the Church says, it is not the soul that shall arise but it is this body: my body, your body — glorified, of course, because Christ is glorified in his body. Concluding this thought, O'Connor says: "It occurs to me that it would never have entered the human consciousness to conceive of purity if we were not to look forward to a resurrection of the body which will be flesh and spirit united in peace," not at war with each other. Flesh and spirit united in peace, the way they are united in peace in the resurrection of Jesus Christ. And so the resurrection of Christ seems to me the high point in the entire law of nature. It took what was destroyed by sin and made it whole again by grace. The resurrection brings flesh and spirit together and restores meaning, hope, and dignity to our lives through faith: because, as St. Paul wrote, "Where sin abounds, grace much more abounds" (Rom. 5:20). What we undid in nature, God redoes by grace.

And so we have choices. Left merely to ourselves, left merely

to nature, we can rage against the dying of the light, as Dylan
Thomas urged his father to do. We can cry out, as does Tenny-
son in his "In Memoriam," against "Nature, red in tooth and
claw" (st. 56, line 15). Or, with the voice of Macbeth's despair-
ing cynicism, we can lament that:

> Life's but a walking shadow, a poor player
> That struts and frets his hour upon the stage,
> And then is heard no more; it is a tale,
> Told by an idiot, full of sound and fury
> Signifying nothing. (V.v.24–28)

Or we can avoid rage and cynicism, facing both life and death
instead with Prospero's gentle stoicism:

> Our revels now are ended. . . .
>   We are such stuff
> As dreams are made on, and our little life
> Is rounded with a sleep.
> (IV.i.148,156–58)

Or we can make the mighty affirmation of faith that rescues
us from rage, despair, or mere resignation.

We can cry aloud and witness to the world. We can witness
to hope. We can witness to the reunion in Christ of flesh and
spirit. With Paul we can writhe beneath the question of deepest human anguish; with him we can shout triumphantly the
affirmation of deepest human hope: "What a wretched man am
I! Who shall deliver me from the body of this death? Thanks
be to God through Jesus Christ our Lord" (Rom. 7:24), because
through his resurrection I have been delivered.

The Third Sunday of Easter

Acts 3:13–15, 17–19 / 1 John 2:1–5 / Luke 24:35–48

■ Today is the third Sunday of Easter. The Church does not say it is the second Sunday *after* Easter but rather calls it the third Sunday *of* Easter. Easter is one great plunge into faith and it lasts for fifty days. These fifty days, the days between the first day of Easter and the last day of Easter (Pentecost, that is), the Church fathers called "the Great Sunday."

All these days are as one great Sunday, exact copies of that first day on which the Lord Jesus appeared. On these Sundays and in the daily liturgies we read these moving, deeply challenging, and in some ways troubling accounts of the various apparitions of Jesus as the Lord, as the Christ. Like us, the disciples were full of fear. Like us, the disciples did not really begin to understand. Like us, the disciples demanded truth. And like us (even after they had had some tangible evidence), they found faith terribly difficult.

Last Sunday, in another account, we read how Thomas doubted this apparition. (The whole story of Thomas is deeply moving.) Thomas had said eight days earlier: "Unless I put my finger in his hands, unless I put my hand into his side, I cannot believe" (John 20:25). Then, on this second evening of his appearance, Jesus called to Thomas: "Thomas, come here. Here are my hands. Put your finger in them. Look at my side. Bring hither your hand. Do not be a nonbeliever. Become a believer" (John 20:27). And Thomas believed, just as the other disciples had come, reluctantly and with great pain, to believe that the Lord was alive again and truly in their midst.

All of these Sundays of Easter and all of these accounts of the appearances of the risen Christ contain a dialectic between faith and doubt. The dialectic is inescapable. The Lord is here apprehended not through mere sight but by a leap of acceptance. He is apprehended in faith. It is no longer Jesus the dusty and itinerant rabbi whom we have with us. It is the glory of God, made manifest in the resurrection. Jesus, the Glory of God, becomes our completion through faith.

Like the disciples we find it hard to accept this. It is beyond human reckoning and beyond human imagining. And yet it is our fulfillment. At the center of the Church's theology we confess that the resurrection of Christ is not an isolated event. "Christ," as St. Paul says, "is the first born from among the dead, the first to be raised up" (Col. 1:18). His resurrection embodies God's plan for the destiny of the human race. Christ is the first born. His being raised up from the dead, his conquering of the tomb, and his share now in the glory of the Father is not his alone. The destiny of Christ is not simply the destiny of Christ. It is our destiny through him. Our God is the God of the living and not a god of the dead. Our God is the God who said to Moses and said again through Jesus: "I desire not death but life." Death, then, for Jesus and for us, is merely a passage; death is not ultimate.

I have been struck recently by the realization that the new bishop of Rome, the chief bishop of the Church, John Paul II, seems to have a great vision of this truth: that Christ is the completion, through his resurrection, of human destiny and of the destiny of history. Marx says that the class struggle is the key to human history and is itself the center of human society as we have come to know it. The opening words of John Paul's first encyclical are these: "Jesus Christ is the center of human history and of human destiny." Given that the pontiff was reared in a Communist country, one must suspect that this affirmation of his encyclical was not indeliberate. John Paul was, it seems, shaping a vision the exact opposite of any Marxist/materialist view of man, of history, or of human destiny.

The glorification of the human race in Jesus Christ; the discovery of man's destiny and meaning in the resurrection of Christ: that is the good news. It cannot be repeated too often. Ours is a resurrection faith. This is the apostolic preaching: Christ is risen. Christ lives. Your sins are forgiven. You must feel peace because no cause for any ultimate fear now exists. We have heard so often from the existentialist philosophers that the great and primordial fear is the fear of nothingness, that is, the fear of death and of annihilation. The great hope, which the gospel erects in opposition to this primal fear, is nothing less than the resurrection of life itself and our promised share in the life of God.

Our promised share in the life of God is the great hope and the great vision, the great joy and the great alleluia which is set before us every day during this solemn day of Easter.

The Sixth Sunday of Easter

Acts 10:25–26, 34–35, 44–48 / 1 John 4:7–10 / John 15:9–17

■ The three great readings in this Sunday's liturgy speak to us of love. The first reading, from the Acts of the Apostles, speaks to us of the love of God which is universal and encompasses all things that the Lord has created. The love and the mercy of God and the acceptance of God is extended, not just to the Jews, but to all of his creation. Nothing that the Lord has created does he despise, and all things that he has created he draws and invites unto himself through his mercy and through his acceptance. This is the good news of our salvation. This is the apostolic message proclaimed in the Acts of the Apostles.

But the second reading from John and the reading from the discourse of Christ to his friends before the Last Supper speak of love in more explicit terms as a commandment. It is only by love, as the saints and the mystics have told us, that we are finally to be judged. And Jesus has said: "By this all men will know that you are my disciples, if you love one another" (John 13:35). So let us meditate upon the meaning of love in the biblical sense.

Now the meaning of this word in the biblical sense, as so many words in the biblical sense, is a sign of contradiction. The love that is here spoken of, the love that is commanded of us,

Heinz Memorial Chapel, 20 May 1979

is in many ways the opposite of that love which the world knows. In this sense Jesus treats "love" exactly as he does "peace." "Peace I bequeath to you; my own peace I give you, a peace the world cannot give; this is my gift to you" (John 14:27). In the biblical understanding of love and in Christ's commandment of love surely the qualifying phrase is: "You must love one another in the way that I have loved you" (John 15:12).

The love that is spoken of here by our Lord stands in eternal opposition to that love spoken of, sung about and lived by many in our culture: the counterfeit of love in the biblical sense. The love of which our culture speaks is a sign, not of emptying out, but of self-seeking. Our culture's notion of love is rooted not in will but in transitory emotion: a love which comes and goes, a love which is irrational, a love which is as easily ended as begun.

I was preaching recently on this notion and suddenly I thought of the words of a wonderful old song by Billie Holiday. (A few of you might remember Billie Holiday.) She had this wonderful song. In her inimitable way she sang, "Love is like a fountain." (I won't try to sing it!) "Love is like a fountain. It turns off and on. And just when you think it's on, baby, it be done and gone." This is the love that the world knows. But in the Christian understanding, love is a commandment.

How does one command an emotion? How does Christ command us to love? Love in this sense, of course, is not an emotion; it is not a transitory thing. It possesses an element of stability and is rooted in the will. We will to love. We must love even what we do not like. We must love people whom we dislike. We must love when disappointment comes. We must love when failure comes, because failure will come. Love is not a fairy story. Love is often difficult and hard. It is attended with all the vicissitudes and stumblings and failures of life, with disappointment and with pain.

I was reminded this morning by one of my colleagues that St. Thomas, in his anatomy of love, discusses mercy.

Misericordia, mercy, is one of love's children. Love, if it be genuine, is always going to call forth the great fruit of mercy from us. Indeed, Thomas says that "insofar as our neighbor is concerned, mercy is the most puissant of all the virtues" ("Sed inter omnes virtutes quae ad proximum pertinent potissima est misericordia," *Summa* II.ii.30.4).

And only to the extent that we are merciful; only to the extent that our love survives disappointment and pain, survives the death of emotion and the total passing of it; only to the extent that it survives, too, the passing of those things which our culture mistakes for love: only to that extent does our love mark us as Christians. It then shows forth the love that God showed forth for us in Jesus Christ.

God is love. And how is his love shown? Through endurance, through loneliness, through abandonment, through suffering, through death. St. Paul in 1 Corinthians (that great, immortal passage) probably describes it as well as it's ever been described: "Love endures all things. Love suffers all things. Love forgives all things. Love is patient. Love is kind. Love is merciful. Love, finally, is all-accepting" (1 Cor. 13:4-8).

All of us learned in our catechism—if we were fortunate enough to have lived in an age when catechism was still studied—that God loves the sinner. He loves us in our sin because he is all-merciful. He accepts us in our weakness. God is not disappointed with us. God (because he is God) knows that to have been a created thing is to have been a disappointing thing. We are all disappointing things. We are disappointing to each other. We have to be a disappointment because we are human. But love triumphs over disappointment.

Much better than Billie Holiday in her wonderful but theologically flawed song, William Shakespeare understood love nearer its biblical sense in his wonderful sonnet, "Let me not to the marriage of true minds admit impediment." Shakespeare understood that to be human is to be a disappointment. But he also understood that to love is to triumph over disappointment.

> Love is not love which alters when it alteration finds
> Nor bends with the remover to remove.
> Oh, no! It is an ever-fixed mark
> That looks on tempests and is never shaken.

The love of God looks upon the tempests of our lives and the love of God is not shaken. To the extent that our love is the love of God as shown forth in Jesus Christ, no matter how weak a reflection of that love it will always be, to that extent our love must be rooted in something deeper than mere emotion. It must not be transitory. It must have the Pauline power to endure all things, suffer all things, be patient, be kind, and, ultimately, bear the great fruit of mercy: because everything that is created is caught up in the mercy of God.

The Twenty-third Sunday in Ordinary Time

Wisdom 9:13–18 / Philemon 9–10, 12–17 / Luke 14:25–33

— Today, being the first Sunday of the term, provides us all an excellent opportunity to remind ourselves what it means to be a Christian and why we come here together. We can remind ourselves, too, what we who are members of this Oratory university parish might hope to understand together and learn together and accomplish together through the praise of God in his worship and through our friendship with each other.

The words that Simon Peter once said to Jesus are words that all of us must feel when we come in contact with the holy. "Depart from me. I am a sinner" (Luke 5:8). In the Gloria we sing the praises of Christ, saying: "You alone are the Holy One. You alone are the Lord." In the presence of the holy, we feel nothing so much as our own unworthiness. Our first temptation is not to grasp it but to flee from it, to feel that such a chasm exists between God and us, between our limitations and God's might, between our selfishness and God's generosity, between our weakness and God's strength, between our sin and God's holiness, that we can only cry out: "Depart from me. I am a sinner," as did Peter in the presence of his Lord.

How dare we approach the holy in all of our sins? All of us are conscious that we are sinners. To be in the human condi-

Heinz Memorial Chapel, 7 September 1980

tion is to be in the condition of sin. In fact, God's mercy begins with our sin. As St. Paul so marvelously proclaims, "Here is a saying that you can rely on and nobody should doubt that Christ Jesus came into the world to save sinners" (1 Tim. 1:15). As Jesus himself said in another place: "I have come, not to call the just but to call sinners" (Matt. 9:13). St. Paul, speaking of himself, says: "I myself am the greatest of sinners; and if mercy has been shown to me, it is because Jesus Christ meant to make me the greatest evidence of his inexhaustible patience for all the other people who would later have to trust in him to come to eternal life" (1 Tim. 1:15–16).

God deals with us paradoxically. And the great Christian paradox is that God grasped us and loved us and accepted us in our sin. John says in his first letter: "To say that we have never sinned is to call God a liar" (1:10). The assembly of Christians is an assembly of hopeful and rejoicing sinners. It is not the assembly of the just or the "religious," as the world understands the "religious." It is a center of weak and maimed men and women, constantly falling, often doubting, often in darkness, beset with all manner of infirmity — sensuality, selfishness, all manner of self-seeking, standing a bit and then falling, crawling more often than walking, but attempting in all this to crawl toward God, and crawling and falling with hope because the power of God is made most manifest in his dealings with sinners.

To know this is to know the beginning of the good news. The good news, we come to realize, is not a reward for virtue. On the contrary, the good news is a sustainer in the midst of darkness and sin. It is strength in weakness. It is the water that we find in the desert of our lives. It is the shade that we find in the heat of our existence. That is what the good news is. You aren't just in the desert. You aren't just in the heat. You aren't just weak. You are sheltered. You are fed. You may hope. Your own humanity, with all that this implies, need not oppress you because God sustains you. And we have need of God and we come to him in confidence and in hope when we are most aware of our need of him, which is when we are most aware of our weakness and our sin.

If any of you is truly righteous, which I doubt; if any of you is truly strong, which I doubt; if any of you feels no need of God because of your virtue, which is unlikely; then don't bother coming to church. You can live unto yourselves. But if you are weak, if you are foolish, if you are unfaithful, come to the heart of Jesus Christ where the patience and the mercy of God is shown forth. And do not say like Peter: "Depart from me, Lord, I am a sinner," but hear the words of Jesus to Peter: "Do not be afraid." Cast aside your fear, Peter. Put your trust and your hope in me.

To us Jesus says: Come together as a hoping, rejoicing community of believing sinners and look beyond your present condition to a mighty kingdom which has been prepared for you.

The Twenty-sixth Sunday in Ordinary Time

Numbers 11:25–29 / James 5:1–6 / Mark 9:38–43, 47–48

■ Doubtless one could make a case that the parable of the prodigal son is one of the most moving, one of the most beautiful, one of the most profound in all of the gospels. As much or more than any other single story in the New Testament, it announces the heart of the gospel, which is forgiveness.

Before the public ministry of Jesus, John came preaching a good news of repentance and reconciliation. What John prophesied, Jesus fulfilled. In Jesus Christ we are reconciled to each other because we have first been reconciled to our Father. All of our sins are forgiven. There is nothing we can do which will finally cut us off from grace unless we ourselves close our hearts in hatred or in despair. God, the image of openness and of open-heartedness, despises nothing that he has made. All that he has made is redeemed in Christ. All is reconciled in Christ. Those who bear Christ's name must, above all, be ministers of peace. If we are not ministers of peace, nothing else matters. To believe in Christ is to be a minister of reconciliation, a minister of forgiveness.

First of all, we have to forgive ourselves. No one is excused. All of us need to be forgiven; all of us need to forgive ourselves. No matter how much denial we use; no matter how much self-

Heinz Memorial Chapel, 30 September 1979

deception we practice — and all of us live large parts of our lives more or less crudely deceiving ourselves — all of us know the darkness deep in our hearts, the darkness that makes life a struggle to let some light in, the light of Christ.

The French poet Baudelaire used to make this prayer: "God, grant that I may look into my heart and not hate myself." We have first to forgive ourselves. To forgive ourselves is sometimes the most difficult of all things to do. Yet we can summon the courage to forgive ourselves through our faith in the forgiveness already bestowed upon us in Christ. In the words of St. John: "This is what love I mean: not our love for God, but God's love for us." We are first loved in Christ. St. Paul writes: "While we were yet sinners, God loved us and God forgave us" (Rom. 5:8). You remember the old saying — I think it was first said by Pascal in the seventeenth century — "To understand everything is to forgive everything." God knows and understands our every rising up and our every sitting down. He knows and understands when and why we stand, when and why we fall. Because he understands our deepest longings and our deepest needs, because he understands the emptiness that constantly threatens us, he fills us with his reconciliation and love. This is the great message. This is the great prophecy. In Christ the message is proclaimed. In Christ the prophecy is fulfilled.

And I would say that this is the prophecy that John Paul, the chief pastor of God's Church, journeys around the globe to announce: reconciliation, forgiveness, and the infinite worth of man. In the books he has written and in the addresses he has preached, John Paul II has defined a vision of man's infinite worth, everyone's infinite worth, the criminal's infinite worth, the outcast's infinite worth, the sinner's — and we are all sinners — our infinite worth, because we are loved, accepted, and forgiven in Christ.

I thought of this during the first reading today, the reading from the Book of Numbers. Moses says to the people: "Would that all of God's people were prophets" (Num. 11:29). A religion which is not prophetic, a religion which merely conforms to the age and supports the prejudices of the age is a counterfeit religion. If religion is not challenging to our deepest prejudices, to the false gods we all create in our lives, to the dubious ends to which we put our energies, to the idolatries of the culture, then it is not authentic religion. Religion must be prophetic. It must speak a word — the sometimes hard word of reconciliation and forgiveness — to a world which is tearing itself apart by unforgiveness and by division. It must speak a word of hope, of infinite hope, to peoples who do not value themselves and who create for themselves false gods — the gods of nationalism, the gods of race, the gods of a material culture cut off from ultimate value, the gods of ugliness and triviality in art and music and literature. They so surround us that these gods inevitably brush against our lives with their corrupting touch.

Religion and those who speak in the name of religion must prophesy against all the dark and corrupt gods of our age. Religion must speak a prophecy of hope and of forgiveness, of the infinite beauty which is God and of the infinite meaning which is God.

Such prophecy is the special mission of the pope: to be a prophet and to challenge our culture. Not just to challenge the culture of Communist China or the culture of the Soviet Union; it's easy to challenge a culture which is officially atheist. But, more importantly and more subtly, to challenge the assumed and practical atheism of our lives and of our culture. To challenge our divisions, our hatreds, our idolatries, our trivialities: this is the word and prophecy of Christ.

As the pope journeys today in Ireland and tomorrow in our

The Twenty-eighth Sunday in Ordinary Time

Wisdom 7:7–11 / Hebrews 4:12–13 / Mark 10:17–30

— "The word of God cuts like a two-edged sword," so says the letter to the Hebrews. "The word of God is alive and active" (Heb. 4:12). The word of the Lord teaches us the spirit of wisdom and of discernment. It orders our values. It gives perspective and direction to our lives. The search after God is the search after wisdom. Thus we beseech the Lord to send his Holy Spirit, the spirit of wisdom. Only with his wisdom, not our own, can we truly be wise. We pray too for the gift of discernment, of distinguishing.

In the Book of Wisdom we read: "I prayed and the spirit of understanding was granted unto me. I called and the spirit of wisdom came to me. I preferred wisdom to scepters and thrones. I counted wisdom greater than any gem because all other things pass, but wisdom does not cease and in her hands lies uncounted wealth" (Wis. 7:7–8). One of the ancient names given to God is "wisdom," "holy wisdom," *Sancta Sophia*. The search after God is the search after wisdom. Such wisdom as we search for is not a learned thing but is rather a matter of grace and of intuition: a gift of discernment. In wisdom resides the power to see through mere appearance and to grasp the substance, that power which, according to Sophocles, allows a person "to see

Heinz Memorial Chapel, 14 October 1979

life whole." This will mean the power to see life, if we are Catholics and Christians, under the species of eternity and in the light of God's revealed word.

Every time we hear the word of God, we listen to a revelation from the seat of wisdom itself — transcending all cultures, transcending all centuries, transcending history and time, transcending the poor limitations of our own existence. Such revelations reveal us to ourselves. They allow us to know who we are, to know that we are complex, and to know that we are full of contradictions. All of us are weak, but we are at the same time strong. All of us are poor, but we are at the same time rich. All of us are hungry, but we are at the same time filled. All of us are thirsty, but we are at the same time refreshed with the water which, in Jesus' words to the Samaritan woman at the well, springs up within us by the power of the Spirit and unto eternal life.

To live in the spirit of the Christian centuries, to live in the spirit of scripture is to cease to be a partial human being. It is to know that we are not merely the playfools of time. That we are not merely the victims of our particular circumstance in life, whatever that circumstance might be. It is to know that the power of God shows itself forth in an infinite variety of ways. Theology is a matter of finding God in the least expected of places: in the outcasts and in the lame and in halt. Theology is a matter of finding God even in our own weakness. St. Paul cried out, "I give thanks to God for my weakness because in my weakness the power of Christ and of his forgiveness dwells within me" (2 Cor. 12:9–10). Theology is a matter of seeing God in death because through death comes ultimate victory and resurrection.

It is wisdom and theology to know that the merely partial is the most persistent and perhaps the worst enemy of wisdom and of God. We are all, of course, prisoners of partial things, of our own intellectual discipline, of our own professions, and, yes, of our own religion. Be it our church, be it our profession, be it our particular moment in history, be it our own particular cultural prejudices, we are tempted to read the few things we can see for the whole which we cannot see. We are tempted to mistake the prejudices of our own time for some breakthrough of wisdom. The nineteenth-century man in many instances mistook the vision of material progress for the arrival of some utopia, the inevitability of human progress. Psychologism, as it has been called, mistakes psychological perception for wisdom. All these things are partial.

Remember what St. Paul says: "We see now as through a glass darkly. Finally, we shall see face to face and finally we shall know God as we are known by him" (1 Cor. 13:12). Now all is partial. The search after wisdom and the attempt to pray is our search and our attempt to break through from the partial to the whole, from the temporal to the eternal.

God deliver us from the partial parts of our lives. God give us moments in which we break through to those larger things. God give us, at last, the great moment in which we break through to the ultimate thing we haltingly call God.

The Thirty-second Sunday in Ordinary Time

1 Kings 17:10–16 / Hebrews 9:24–28 / Mark 12:38–44

— St. Paul instructs us, "Be imitators of God." How would we dare to even attempt to imitate God? I think at least a partial answer — and all of our answers when we speak of religion are always partial — at least a partial answer is contained in today's readings which speak of generosity and openness and love.

The first lesson from the Book of Kings tells of the generosity of the poor woman toward the prophet Elijah. The second lesson from the Epistle to the Hebrews speaks of the overwhelming generosity of Christ who out of love gave himself up to suffering and death and by his generosity raised up a fallen world. Through generosity creation was made open again unto God. In the third lesson from the gospel we hear the story of that generous poor woman who gave all she had so that God's temple might be richly adorned.

The name of God is always guessed at, but I can think of one philosophical attempt to describe God and one poetic attempt, both of which involve generosity and love. In the *Summa*, St. Thomas tells us that God is that ultimate goodness whose very nature it is to pour itself forth. "It is the nature of good-

Heinz Memorial Chapel, 11 November 1979

ness," St. Thomas says, "to diffuse itself." Goodness cannot be contained within itself. Goodness is openness. Goodness is generosity. We are called upon to be open. We are called upon to make some attempt, however poor, to imitate God. In St. John's first epistle he tells us, "If anyone says that he loves God, but does not love his neighbor, then that person is a liar, because a man who does not love the brother whom he can see cannot love God whom he has never seen" (4:20). "God is love; those who abide in love abide in God and God abides in them" (4:16).

I think many of us were raised in a traditional Catholic piety which forgot this. When we thought of sin, we thought of sin in biological terms, sexually. We thought of sin in legalistic terms. I remember the kind of confession one heard every Saturday when I was first a priest fifteen years ago. It usually involved the breaking of some law: I missed mass on Sunday; I ate meat on Friday; I had impure thoughts. Such confessions missed the nature of sin. The nature of sin is selfishness. Selfishness lies at the heart of sin. Lack of generosity lies at the heart of sin. The reason, I suppose, that sexuality and sexual acts are so open to having in them the nature of sinfulness is that sexuality of its very nature invites exploitation of others. It invites infidelity. It invites selfishness and lack of generosity.

Sin is part of all our lives to the extent that we are ungenerous, to that extent we do not imitate God who is love. St. Paul says: "You must be generous to others because God in Christ has first been generous to you. While we were yet unlovable, God loved us." God accepted us and God invites us to a share in his own generosity, to share in his own openness and to share in his own forgiveness. "Love is patient. Love is kind. Love is forgiving" (1 Cor. 13:4). Love ultimately understands all things. Understanding all things like God, love accepts all things. Noth-

The Feast of St. Philip Neri

Philippians 4:4–9 / John 17:20–26

━ The feast of our father, St. Philip Neri, is a significant day not only because it is the solemnity of that most lovable (many think) of all saints, that most charismatic of all saints, but also because it is a day that for some of us has rich memories and for all of us who love the Oratory has great importance.

Twenty years ago today, when we were all much younger, six of us came together (four priests, two laymen of whom I was then one) to meet at the home of that great man, Bishop (later Cardinal) Wright, to help him fulfill a dream of his. The dream was the Oratory. The dream was to bring together a community of friends in the spirit of the Oratory, a spirit of friendship, openness, liberality, acceptance, support, and love: to bring all these things together and to bring them together especially in the tradition of John Henry Newman, that greatest of all St. Philip's sons. To bring all these things together: openness, love of learning, love of the arts, love (above all) of the Church, the Holy Catholic Church: to bring these together to serve the great secular universities here in Oakland — the University of Pittsburgh and Carnegie-Mellon University and Chatham College. And during these years some have remained and some have gone and a few have died, but the essence, the original vision, remains.

Heinz Memorial Chapel, 26 May 1981

It is an Oratorian vision; it is a Newmanian vision; and, most fundamentally I would hope, it is a Catholic Christian vision: to love the word of God, to love the liturgy of the Church, to love serving and knowing each other, to try to render a service to each other and to the Church and to these universities in that spirit of love, of openness, and of tolerance which characterized St. Philip Neri. This is the gift that we can make to the Church in Pittsburgh. These twenty years we have tried to make just such a gift: with whatever failures along the way and, I hope to God, with some successes.

St. Philip is that most congenial of saints for all of these things. Philip, to quote Newman, "was a man who loved and served his times." And in a famous passage from Newman's lecture on "The Duty of the Church Toward Knowledge" in *The Idea of the University*, Newman wrote of St. Philip and of Philip's peculiar genius and because of this peculiar genius Philip's perennial relevance to those who seek to build bridges between the gospel and the world. "St. Philip," Newman wrote, addressing those undergraduates in Dublin a hundred and thirty years ago, "St. Philip Neri was raised up to do a work most special and peculiar in the Church": not to be a judge of his times, not to be a Jerome Savonarola, though Philip had a true admiration for him; not to be a great reformer, like St. Charles Borromeo, his contemporary, though in the "beaming countenance" of Charles Borromeo Philip recognized the aureole of a saint; not to be an Ignatius of Loyola, wrestling with the foe, though Philip was termed the "bell of the Society of Jesus" so many men did he send there; not to be a St. Francis Xavier, to go to far places to give his life for the gospel and for Jesus Christ, even though Philip longed to die for Christ. No, Philip's mission was a tranquil one. And tranquility is the key to the Oratory.

Philip preferred tranquility, to cast his net into the stream of his times in order to gain others for Christ. Philip preferred to yield to the currents of science, of literature, of music, and of art which were flowing freely during his day and to sweeten and to sanctify them and to love them and thus to make and keep very good what man without God can spoil.

And so the key to St. Philip and to our mission, the key to the Oratory and to whatever future we have is the love of some very basic things: first of all, love of the Church. To love the Holy Catholic Church, who is our mother, and to seek to express that love by bringing the best that we have to her service, which is what we try to do (with whatever failures) in the tradition of Philip Neri. And in loving the Church to love the world because the Church exists not to judge the world but to save the world, to comfort the world in its darkness, to cast light into the world. To love the world — to use a phrase of Dietrich Bonhoeffer — to love the world in a spirit of "holy worldliness." To love all that is good, all that is beautiful and all that is true in our times, in our culture and to bring these things to the service of the Church. To love literature, to love science, to love music, to love art — all of them, manifestations of the beauty of God himself and his wisdom. To love the liturgy of the Church — this worship which is the presence of God and the glimpse of paradise and of God's kingdom among us even now. To love the word of God and to preach it in season and out of season, day in and day out, and to make it our constant meditation. And to love friendship because the Oratory does not exist by rule or by discipline the way religious orders do. The Oratory exists by friendship, by mutuality, by forbearance, and by giving. This is the unique genius of St. Philip and of the Oratory.

To recall us to our vision on this our twentieth anniversary, I can think of nothing better to quote than words from our founder, Bishop John Wright, Cardinal Wright — words that the then-bishop of Pittsburgh spoke from this pulpit when he preached here on an earlier St. Philip's Day. He recalled us to what we are, to what our mission is, and to what our vision should be. Bishop Wright said: "The mission of the Oratory is to preach the faith in a way worthy of a university community and within the university community to celebrate the liturgy, the worship of the Church, with a dignity and a beauty worthy of the mystery and profundity of what we celebrate."

Let us, all of us who love the Oratory, who love St. Philip, and who love Cardinal Newman rededicate ourselves to these things today.

The Feast of All Saints

Revelation 7:2-4, 9-14 / 1 John 3:1-3 / Matthew 5:1-12

■ The Solemnity of All Saints is surely one of the great solemnities in the calendar of the Church. Not only is it ancient in its origins but also and more importantly it is profound in its implications and universal in its application. It is our feast.

This is not the feast of those plaster figures we see in religious houses. Saints vested in plaster uphold and show forth some standard of behavior that is well beyond the reach of most, if not all of us. But it is the feast of all of us — it is our feast — it is the feast of the worst sinners who know their need of God. "Blessed," we can say, "are those who know their need of God; they shall inherit the earth." It is the feast of God touching us and we have all been touched. It is the feast of the generosity of God and all of us have felt his generosity. It is the feast of all saints and all of us, no matter how sinful we may be on occasion in our lives, are saints. Because a saint is a member of that new creation which was purchased at a great price by Christ and bestowed on us as free gift in the Church and in the sacraments and in the promise of eternal life which is their fruit. And so I say to all of us: Congratulations. It is our feast, the Feast of All Saints!

Heinz Memorial Chapel, 1 November 1981

Some saints have been weak. Some saints have been wretched. Some saints, I'm sure, have been most unpleasant people to deal with or live with. Some saints have been impatient. Some saints have been short-tempered. Just as most of us have been all of these things and continue to be, so the saints once were. But we are all saints because we are all reborn in baptism and because we all partake of the table of the Lord and through that table look forward to the banquet of eternal life, our future inheritance.

The Feast of All Saints is the feast of God's mercy. It is the feast that reminds us of what St. Paul reminded the Corinthians when he wrote to them and said: "When you hold these meetings, it is not the Lord's supper that you are eating, since when the time comes to eat, everyone is in such a hurry to start his own supper that one person goes hungry while another is getting drunk. . . . What am I to say to you? Congratulate you? I cannot congratulate you on this" (1 Cor. 11:20–22). And yet Paul calls all the Corinthians "saints" because they are all members of that new creation which was created by Christ in his cross and in his death and in his resurrection.

That is the first profound meaning of this feast which applies to all of us. Secondly, there is no affirmation in the Church's creed more profound in its immediate meaning to us and even in its significance for the larger world than our belief in the communion of saints. "I believe in the communion of saints." Just as the ancient hymn says that in Christ there is no east and west but all come together in Christ, so come together all manner and matter of men and women. And time itself, that enemy of us all, that inescapable reality of which we are all afraid – time in its passage and in its consequences – time is overcome. Christ conquers death and along with death he conquers time.

Because Christ has overcome time, we are one with the saints who went before us. And by way of anticipation and prevenient grace we are one with the saints who will come after us. We form the Church, that great community of those who have been selected by God and who have been called by grace and not by good works already accomplished. In his letter to the Romans, Paul says: "By faith we are judged righteous and at peace with God since it is by faith and through Jesus that we have entered this state of grace in which we can boast about looking forward to God's Glory" (Rom. 5:1–2). We have nothing of our own to boast of. The gift of God has called us to glory. We are all the signs of God's gift which is salvation. And we are all united together in saintliness in a way that the world can never unite us, in a bond that cannot be overcome by death, that cannot be overcome by any temporal separation.

We belong to the saints who knew Jesus in his life; we belong to the apostles. We belong to the saints whom we might pick out to be our models through the centuries. We belong to the saints who will come after us. We may fail in our own lives; saints fail. A saint is not a plastic thing. A saint is a real thing, with all the failures and limitations of finitude, of reality. And we all partake in that. We partake in the communion of saints with the mighty hope that all our weaknesses can be overcome in Christ. And they are overcome in his grace. And that is the meaning of the profound doctrine of the communion of saints. We are all united together, not through our own efforts, but through God's great gift — bestowed through history, scattered through history and uniting all of us in a destiny we did not make and could not possibly make ourselves, but which has been made for us by Almighty God. And so we praise God in his saints.

And we pray, too, that the fruit of sanctity will be ours. Because, having been made saints through baptism, we are called

William Clancy: Significant Dates

1922   Born in Detroit, Michigan, on December 21, as he
            liked to point out, the longest night of the year.
1945–46   Graduated from the University of Detroit with both
            a B.A. and an M.A. in English literature.
1946–48   Pursued doctoral studies in English literature at the
            University of Michigan in Ann Arbor.
1948–50   Assorted editorial posts in England and Germany.
1950–52   Taught at Notre Dame University in the English
            Department.
1952–56   Writer, assistant editor, and associate editor of
            Commonweal.
1956–57   Religion editor, *Newsweek.*
1957–60   Founding editor and editor, *Worldview.*
1957–59   Special consultant, Center for the Study of Demo-
            cratic Institutions.
1961   Founding member of the Pittsburgh Oratory.
1962–65   Studied theology at Christ Church, Oxford.
1964   Ordained a Roman Catholic priest by Cardinal John J.
            Wright in Heinz Memorial Chapel of the University
            of Pittsburgh.
1968   Elected provost of the Pittsburgh Oratory.
1968–82   Provost of the Pittsburgh Oratory and pastor of the
            University Oratory of the Holy Spirit.
1982   Died January 6, the Feast of the Epiphany, at the
            Oratory.